Spencer TRACY

Spencer Tracy

Alison King

Crescent Books
New York

This 1992 edition published by Crescent
Books,
distributed by Outlet Book Company, Inc.,
a Random House Company,
40 Engelhard Avenue,
Avenel, New Jersey 07001

Produced by
Brompton Books Corporation
15 Sherwood Place
Greenwich, CT 06830

ISBN 0-517-06705-6

8 7 6 5 4 3 2 1

Printed and bound in Hong Kong

Page 1: Tracy in *The Sea of Grass* (1947), in which he
co-starred with Katharine Hepburn.

Page 2: On his Encino ranch with his Irish setter –
Spencer's own Irish lineage is unmistakable.

Page 4/5: With Katharine Hepburn in a scene from
The State of the Union, regarded by some as the best
film they made together.

Contents

1. The Early Years, *1900-1930* 6

2. The First Films, *1930-1935* 16

3. The Movie Star, *1935-1941* 28

4. Katharine Hepburn, *1942-1950* 38

5. The Father Figure, *1950-1958* 54

6. The Stanley Kramer Films,
   1959-1967 64

Filmography 74

Index 79

Acknowledgments 80

Chapter 1
THE EARLY YEARS
1900-1930

Below: This publicity still of Tracy was taken in 1940 when he was at the height of his first success at Metro Goldwyn Mayer.

Opposite: A younger Tracy.

WHEN Spencer Tracy first tried to find a part in motion pictures in the late 1920s, he was told that he was neither good-looking enough to play a leading man nor ugly enough to play a villain. Tracy had none of the classic good looks of his contemporary Clark Gable and already, at the age of 28, his face was deeply lined. When he

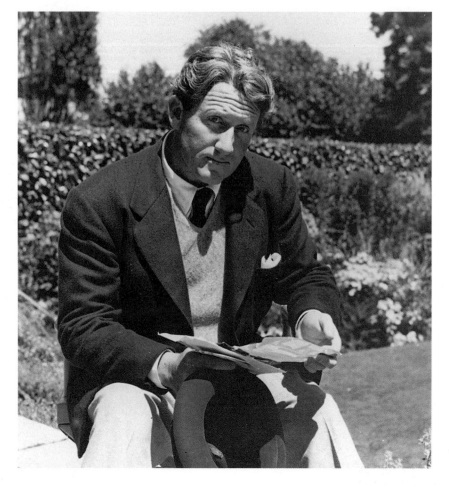

approached casting agents they judged him on his looks and not his acting ability. Once the film director John Ford had seen him act, however, it was a different story. In mid-1930, Ford was in New York looking for actors to play in his new film *Up the River*. Spencer Tracy was appearing in the play *The Last Mile* on Broadway. Ford had intended to watch a different play on each evening of the week he was in New York. Instead he was so impressed by Tracy that he returned to see him in *The Last Mile* for six consecutive evenings. Needless to say, Tracy was offered a part in *Up the River* and so began an amazing career in films that was to last over 30 years.

During this career he was hailed as one of the greatest screen actors of his time by some of the other great actors of the day, including Laurence Olivier, Humphrey Bogart and Jimmy Cagney. His supreme acting talents are still appreciated by thousands of people today as the great films in which he starred appear time and again on our television and cinema screens. These include his early Oscar-winning films, *Captains Courageous* and *Boys' Town*, the films of his long-lasting partnership with Katharine Hepburn, such as *Woman of the Year* and *Adam's Rib*, and his last great films directed by Stanley Kramer, *Inherit the Wind*, *It's a Mad Mad Mad Mad World*, *Judgment at Nuremberg* and *Guess Who's Coming to Dinner*.

Yet despite his huge success as an actor, Tracy was not a happy man. Throughout his working life he fought a battle against alcoholism, caused partly perhaps by the dichotomy of his character. By turns he could be generous, quiet and thoughtful and then loud and bad-tempered. It is hard to say what

caused these huge swings of mood, for he did not allow many people close enough to him to find out. Even his partner for over 25 years, Katharine Hepburn, could not explain why he led such an unsettled life.

He was born in Milwaukee on April 5, 1900. His father, John, was an Irish Catholic businessman who, on the night of Spencer's birth, celebrated by getting drunk in Milwaukee's Irish bars. His mother, Carrie, was a gentler character, a Protestant, whose family was descended from the colonial Browns of New England, one of whom founded the Ivy League Brown University in Providence, Rhode Island. Her family felt that she had married beneath her but she was obviously attracted to John Tracy's masculinity and adventurous spirit, qualities Spencer was to inherit. The difference in their parents' religion did not cause Spencer or his older brother, Carroll, any problems; there was no doubt that they would both be raised as Catholics. His father was a devout Catholic who would have been proud if one of his sons had become a priest. Later on in life this may have been a source of tension for Spencer, for he never really regarded acting as a 'serious' profession and felt

that he should have tried to fulfill his father's ambitions.

There was little precedent in his family for working in the theater. His father was general sales manager of the Sterling Motor Truck Company. The family were relatively prosperous and during Spencer's early years he lived in a comfortable house on Prospect Avenue, Milwaukee, a pleasant, tree-lined street in a cosmopolitan part of the city where there were few Irish but many Germans and Poles. Unfortunately, the comfort of Spencer's home life did not prevent him from getting into numerous scrapes; he was a difficult child who hated school and was often involved in fights. He would journey both to the wealthy Irish stronghold of Shorewood in the north of the city and to the poorer Irish neighborhoods in the west and south, in order to pick fights with his fellow Irishmen.

It was on one of these forays into the south side that he made two of his childhood friends, 'Ratty' and 'Mousy' Donovan, whose father owned a saloon. With them, Spencer would hide under the bar in the saloon, listening to the conversation of the customers. Although this was hardly the ideal education for a teen-

Below: A rare photograph of Tracy with his wife Louise and son John at a polo match, taken in Los Angeles in 1939, the year before he met Katharine Hepburn. Polo was an obsession of Tracy's at this time, partly in response to his frustration with the unsatisfactory roles he was offered.

SPENCER TRACY

age boy, it certainly improved his understanding of human nature, as he listened to the earthy chatter of the drinkers at the bar. His frequent truanting from school to roam the streets with Ratty and Mousy, and his aggressive nature, caused Tracy to be expelled from several schools. He claimed later that he attended 15 schools before he finally graduated.

It was during his early teens that he first showed an interest in films, becoming an aficionado of silent movies. He would put on shows based on the films he had seen in the basement of the house in the less affluent west side of Milwaukee where the family moved when John Tracy suffered one of his financial setbacks. Spencer both wrote and performed in these shows. Unfortunately several of them ended in fights as the young customers, who had paid one cent each to watch, rioted, complaining about the quality of the scripts. Carroll had to play the role of his brother's bodyguard, protecting him from the larger assailants, a function he continued to perform throughout Spencer's life, rescuing him from bars and hotels when he went on one of his drinking sprees. Then he was protecting Spencer mainly from himself and his alcoho-

Left: Tracy as a boy. He was a disruptive child, disliking and frequently truanting from school, and was expelled several times.

Below: Tracy pictured shortly after he had signed a contract with Metro Goldwyn Mayer. Slip Along was his favorite polo pony, and he spent much of his spare time engaged in this dangerous sport.

lism, rather than the anger of disappointed teenagers.

Spencer's uneven school career continued until 1917, when he was enrolled in the expensive Marquette Academy with an Irish friend, Bill O'Brien, who was later to change his name to Pat O'Brien. The two boys were destined to be friends for a long time, as their careers followed similar paths. Spencer settled down at the Marquette Academy more than at any of his other schools, but this was 1917, the year America entered the First World War; inevitably, Spencer wanted to take part in the action. He had inherited his father's adventurous spirit, and to a young man of 17 the war was too exciting a prospect to miss. So with his brother, Carroll, and Pat he joined the Navy. His hopes for adventure were thwarted, however, and he passed his short time in the Navy at the Norfolk naval yard in Virginia, cleaning ships and spending lonely hours on watch. Later he said that, during this time, he brooded about how much he had disappointed his parents and how he 'had to get his life in order.'

On his discharge from the Navy Spencer failed to settle back into school life at the Marquette Academy. In 1919 he enrolled in the Northwestern Military and Naval Academy, Lake Geneva, Wisconsin, perhaps in an attempt to get back to the kind of life he led in the Navy. It was here that he met Kenneth Edgers, a cultured, sophisticated boy from Seattle who was to have a profound effect on Spencer's life. Kenneth was bound for Ripon College, one of the most prestigious colleges in the midwest; Spencer admired his new friend so much that he decided to follow him to Ripon, and it was here that his career as an actor began.

Above: Tracy looking much older than his twelve years. His family were reasonably prosperous and ran their own car.

Right: Tracy with the other members of the Ripon College debating team. It was while he was on tour with the team that he auditioned successfully for the American Academy of Dramatic Art in New York.

Bumby,   Tracy,   MacDougall

Eastern Debating Team

Above: Tracy with his mother, Mrs Carrie B Tracy. Widowed before Tracy started his Hollywood career, she moved to Los Angeles to be closer to her son.

Professor J Clark Graham, the Ripon College drama teacher, invited him to audition for a part in the annual college play, *The Truth*. He impressed Professor Graham both with his resonant voice and his amazing memory. He was the only one at audition who did not need to read the script, for he had already memorized it, and this ability to memorize lines quickly was constantly to impress his colleagues during his career. Needless to say, he was given the leading role. He went on to win parts in other college productions and his powers of delivery also enabled him to gain a place in the college debating team. It was while he was on a tour with the debating team that, with the support of Professor Graham, he auditioned for the American Academy of Dramatic Art in New York. Franklin Havers Sargent, the founder of the Academy, was present at the audition and offered Spencer a place immediately; in April, 1922, he began his course at the Academy.

In New York he shared a room with his old friend from Milwaukee, Pat O'Brien, who was also a student at the Academy. Life was hard for the two young men: they both lived on the thirty dollars a month veterans' benefit they received from the Government, surviving mainly on a diet of pretzels, rice and water and wearing one another's clothing to keep laundry costs down. Spencer never asked for help from his father, who disapproved of his acting aspirations. When he graduated from the Academy in March, 1923 life became even harder, for his veteran's benefit from the Navy also came to an end. For several months Spencer struggled on and in June 1923, when he had almost given up hope of finding an acting job and was thinking of returning to Milwaukee, he managed to get work in a new stock company being formed by Leonard Wood Junior in White Plains, New York.

On the train Tracy took from Grand Central Station to White Plains was his future wife, Louise Treadwell. She was also on her way to join the Leonard Wood stock company. At 27, four years older than Tracy, she was an established actress and was to take the role of leading lady in the play *The Man Who Came Back*. She had already played the lead in a tour of a well-known play called *Nothing But the Truth* and had a secondary role in *The Pigeon* on Broadway. Louise belonged to a respectable Episcopalian family in New Castle, Pennsylvania. The great influence in her life thus far had been her mother, Alliene, who had en-

Right: George M Cohan,
American actor, playwright
and producer, who was a
major influence on Tracy's
early career. Impressed by
Tracy's playing of a small
part in *Yellow* (1926), he
wrote *The Baby Cyclone*
specifically with him in
mind.

escaped by attending Lane Erie College for
Women, from which she graduated in 1917.
She had also had several other jobs, including
one as a reporter on the local New Castle
newspaper and another as a teacher. In 1919,
after the death of her mother and perhaps feel-
ing guilty about not fulfilling her mother's
ambitions for her, she returned to the stage.

Tracy introduced himself to Louise on the
platform at White Plains station, and so their
courtship began. He was immediately impressed by Louise, not only because of her
striking looks but also because of her greater
acting experience. He had had little experience of women so far in his life, never
having the money to take them out. He
quickly became infatuated with her and she
with him. She later said of Tracy:

I loved him because he was so earnest, so attentive
and such a good actor. With a single line, boomed
out in that strong voice of his, he could instantly
command the attention of the audience.

She was so impressed that she managed to
arrange for him to be taken on as a part of the
Repertory Theater of Cincinnati, the company she joined after the Leonard Wood company went out of business. It was here that
Tracy proposed and was accepted. They were
married in Cincinnatti on September 12,
1923.

couraged Louise in her stage career. In fact
Alliene had exerted almost too much pressure
on her to pursue a career in the theater, and on
several occasions Louise had rebelled. She had

The first months of their married life were
spent on the road, acting in stock companies,
and this experience provided Tracy with his
apprenticeship as an actor. Stock companies

Right: Tracy (third from
left) as a robot in R.U.R.
(Rossum's Universal
Robots), Karel Capek's
science-fantasy. The play,
in its American premiere,
was staged by the Theater
Guild at the Garrick
Theater in New York. It
was one of Tracy's first
parts after leaving the
Academy of Dramatic Art,
when he was still struggling
to make ends meet.

Left: Spencer and Louise photographed in the early years of his career. The discovery that his son was deaf placed a strain on the marriage, but Louise never failed to support and encourage her husband.

330-spec 68

performed mainly farces and comedies, formula pieces that required a limited amount of scenery and props. They were either based in one of the larger cities or would travel from one town to another. The routine of stock provided an excellent training for many young actors who, at that time, included future stars such as Jeanette MacDonald and Cary Grant. At any one time the company would be performing one play, rehearsing another and learning a third. It gave the young Tracy a discipline he was to maintain until his last days as an actor. To the chagrin of other actors, he always knew his part by the first rehearsal, and usually their parts as well.

Louise continued in stock until the impending birth of the Tracys' first child forced her to give up and move in with Tracy's parents in Milwaukee, where John Tracy was born on June 26, 1924. Meanwhile Tracy carried on in stock alone; by now he had earned a reputation as a reliable, powerful player and it was easier for him to get work. After John's birth he worked with W H Wright's company in Grand Rapids, Michigan. The company's leading lady was Selena Royle, who was one of Tracy's early champions. She said of him:

All Spence had to do was walk on the stage and you knew he belonged there . . . he dominated it. It's difficult to be natural on stage, but it's the only place where Spence was completely natural.

During the winter of 1924/25, Wright's company worked in Brooklyn. Tracy had been growing increasingly lonely without Louise and he managed to persuade her to join him with John. It was here that Tracy discovered that his son was deaf. One Sunday afternoon he was playing with John and to attract his attention he shouted and clapped his hands, but the child did not respond. Louise, who had already discovered John's deafness but had been unable to tell Tracy, had to admit that their son could not hear. Tracy reacted badly to the news and, as Pat O'Brien later recalled, 'went out and got drunk. It was the first big drunk of his life, as far as I know. He was gone for days and finally was found holed up in the St George Hotel there in Brooklyn.' Spencer had even more incentive now to work hard at his career, however, for money would be needed to help John, and in order to make money Spencer needed to be successful as an actor.

Success did not come for a couple of years though, during which time Tracy fell into a depression, most probably caused by his son's deafness. Fathering a disabled son made Tracy feel a failure. He had grown up in a society that placed great store on masculinity and virility. It is likely that he felt John's deafness was somehow his fault. He was unable to voice these feelings, however, or perhaps even admit them to himself. Instead he tried to escape from them by drinking. Alcohol affected his work for the first time when he was drunk during a performance of George M Cohan's *The Song and Dance Man* while with the Trent Theater stock company, New Jersey. He was fired but saved, because nobody could be found to replace him in the middle of the season. He then stayed with the Trent Theater company

until the middle of 1926, when he returned to W H Wright's company in Grand Rapids. By now Tracy was becoming frustrated in stock. He later commented: 'I had done more than fifty plays and a lot of guys, without my talent, were making it on Broadway, while I was still stuck in the sticks.'

Selena Royle, with whom Tracy had worked when he first joined Wright's company, was trying to help him improve his situation. She was now in New York, a success playing *ingénue* roles, and in mid-1926 had just been given the lead role in a new George M Cohan play called *Yellow*. She persuaded Cohan to give Tracy a reading for a part in the play, and he was cast as Jimmy Wilkes, a bank clerk, receiving eighth billing. The part was a highly significant one for Tracy, for it introduced him to George M Cohan, who was to have a great influence on his acting. Tracy later said of Cohan: 'The old master taught me everything I knew about underplaying and timing.' The respect was mutual. Cohan, who had a reputation for being cantankerous and rarely gave compliments, is reputed to have said during a rehearsal of *Yellow*, 'Spencer Tracy, you're the best damn actor I ever saw.'

Yellow ran for about six months, during which time Tracy was elected to membership of the Lambs Club, which he frequented regularly with his friends Pat O'Brien and Lynne Overman. Situated just off Broadway, this had been founded by a group of actors in the nineteenth century and was famous for its conviviality. Louise meanwhile, was growing

Above: Tracy in *The Baby Cyclone*, the play written especially for him by George M Cohan. It was a farce about two couples who constantly quarreled over a pet Pekinese.

Right: A publicity still for *Captains Courageous* (1937) showing Tracy with Freddie Bartholomew, the child actor he so admired. The film tells the story of the relationship that develops between Manuel, a Portuguese fisherman played by Tracy, and Harvey Cheyne, the son of a business tycoon (Bartholomew), whom Manuel rescues after he has been washed off a transatlantic liner.

"Hold it, my lad. We'll talk this over as man to man!" said Manuel.

Rudyard Kipling's CAPTAINS COURAGEOUS

Metro Goldwyn Mayer picture

"We're married, officer... we're only fooling!"

Luise **RAINER** • Spencer **TRACY**

in **BIG CITY**

A Metro-Goldwyn-Mayer Picture

Above: A publicity still for *Big City* (1937), in which Tracy plays a taxi driver.

Right: Tracy with his five-year-old daughter, Susie, in 1939.

restless and wanted to return to acting. When *Yellow* closed Spencer therefore agreed to go back to stock, and the couple rejoined W H Wright's company in Lima, Ohio. Neither of them enjoyed the experience; it was a come-down for Spencer after Broadway and Louise was ill, finding it hard to look after John and act as well. After nine weeks, Cohan wired Spencer to say he was ready to go into produc-tion with *The Baby Cyclone*, a play he had writ-ten specifically for Spencer. The couple returned to New York, where Tracy appeared in *The Baby Cyclone* for six months and then in another Cohan play, *Whispering Friends*. It was during the run of *Whispering Friends* that Tracy's father died of cancer. His parents had moved to New York when his father had been transferred there by General Motors. They had been to see Tracy three times in *The Baby Cyclone* and his father had finally shown approval of Tracy's choice of career, telling him, 'You're doing well, son, at what you've chosen to be your life's work.'

Chapter 2
THE FIRST FILMS
1930-1935

THE death of Tracy's father was followed by an acute bout of insomnia which further deepened the lines on his face. Tracy had none of the classic good looks which the light comedies of the time required of leading men, and Louise encouraged him instead to go for more serious roles which would show off his acting talents. He was not a very good judge of scripts, however, and in 1929 appeared in four plays, all of which were flops. Then in 1930, he agreed to appear in a play called *The Last Mile*, which was very different from the comedies and farces so popular at this time, after the Wall Street Crash of 1929 and the beginning of the Great Depression. The play was based on the true story of a convict

Right: Tracy and Warren Hymer in a still from his first film, *Up the River* (1930). Tracy and Hymer, playing a pair of seasoned criminals, Saint Louis and Dannemora Dan, are pictured in the prison yard ready for the big baseball game.

called Robert Blake, who wrote down his thoughts while he awaited execution on Death Row. Blake's name was changed to Killer Mears in the play, and the part was taken by Tracy. A prison break and a riot were added to the play after a riot erupted in Auburn Prison in upstate New York in January 1930. Tracy thought he had another flop on his hands but the critics did not agree. The play was an overnight success on Broadway and Tracy was hailed as an actor of amazing power.

In 1930 Tracy had finally become a success on Broadway, but he was not to remain there for long. During the run of *The Last Mile*, the director John Ford came to Broadway to sign up actors for a new film that the Fox Film Corporation was making about a prison escape, to be called *Up The River*. As has been related, Ford was so impressed by Tracy that he went to see him six times in *The Last Mile*. He later said: 'More than anything else, I was tantalized by his movement. I don't think many people were ever conscious of Spencer's bodily discipline.' When he had seen Tracy for the third time, he said 'that he had it all . . . the consummate power of an actor.' He signed up Tracy for the film without hesitation.

In the only matinée Ford went to see that week, he spotted another unknown actor whom he also signed for *Up the River*; the actor's name was Humphrey Bogart. Although the two were not to appear in any more films together, they struck up a friendship that was to last until Bogart's death. Tracy was granted

Above: With Claire Luce who plays Judy, a prisoner in the women's section of the jail in *Up the River*.

Left: Spencer with Humphrey Bogart as Steve, a fellow prisoner who is in love with Judy. Once released from prison, Steve is blackmailed by a crooked salesman, Frosby. Once Saint Louis and Dan hear of this they escape from prison to go to Steve's help, save his reputation, and then return to prison.

Right: In action in his favorite sport of polo, riding his own horse Two Socks, just after he had finished making *Mannequin* (1938) with Joan Crawford. After an injury, Tracy was banned by the film studio from playing the sport in case he should hurt himself further. He ignored the ban, however, escaping detection by playing under a pseudonym.

Below: Tracy, Bogart and Claire Luce in *Up the River*.

a leave of absence of six weeks from *The Last Mile* to make *Up The River*, which was completed just in time for him to return to Broadway to honor his commitment. When it was released in October 1930, it was obvious that it was a success. Richard Watts Jr in the *Herald Tribune* clearly thought Tracy had more films to his credit and wrote that Spencer Tracy gave his 'usual' excellent performance. The Fox executives offered Tracy a long term contract but he was unable to take it up until November 1930, when *The Last Mile* completed its run. He was then signed up to Fox with a salary of $1,200 a week, and the Tracys moved to Hollywood.

There was little evidence of the Depression in Hollywood. In New York it had been very evident, with theater attendance plummeting and unemployment, particularly among actors, growing. In contrast Hollywood was booming. Expensive cars lined the streets and parties were extravagant. The area was still relatively undeveloped, however, and much of the San Fernando Valley was covered with bean fields and orange groves. The Tracys began to settle into Hollywood life, with Louise dedicating herself to John, teaching him to lipread and to talk, while Tracy discovered polo and spent many hours playing. Several of his fellow drinkers from the Lambs Club, including Pat O'Brien, Frank Morgan

Above: With George Raft in Spencer's second film, *Quick Millions* (1931). He plays 'Bugs' Raymond, a protection racketeer who decides that he wants to marry a society lady, Dorothy Stone, but she is in love with someone else and his plans are thwarted by his own henchmen, who prevent the marriage.

Left: Tracy with some of the other Hollywood stars who shared his passion for polo: from left, Leslie Howard, Will Rogers and Johnny Mack Brown. Carole Lombard is presenting the trophies to the winning team, the actors, who beat the production team. Note the contrast between the dapper Englishman Howard and the disheveled Tracy in his topcoat.

and William Boyd, had also been lured to Hollywood. As he became more frustrated with the roles he was given, Tracy turned more to the diversions Hollywood offered. When he first arrived in Hollywood gangster films were popular; Edward G Robinson and James Cagney were both appearing as gangsters for Warner Brothers, and Fox also needed a 'tough guy'. Tracy was to fulfil ths role. This reassured Tracy, who was always worried about his looks: to play a gangster, an actor did not have to be good-looking. His next film was called *Quick Millions*; Tracy played 'Bugs' Raymond, an amiable, basically honest but ambitious truck driver, corrupted during the Depression by money and the lust for power. Today it is regarded as a near-classic gangster movie, with Tracy in his first starring part, and at the time the reviews were favorable, but it was less successful at the box office.

The next part assigned to Tracy was not that of a tough guy; he was told that it was to be a comedy called *A Girl in Every Port*, a title later changed to *Goldie*. After reading the scripts, Tracy confronted the head of the studio, Winfield Sheehan, demanding to know what happened to his tough guy role. This was to be the

first of many arguments between Sheehan and Tracy. After Sheehan explained that gangster films were losing their popularity and that Tracy should not get himself typed, Tracy set to work on the film relatively obediently. His co-star was a young Jean Harlow and during the making of *Goldie* he is reputed to have given her advice that greatly improved her acting. He stopped Harlow during rehearsals, saying, 'Jean, why are you acting so God-damned phony?' He told her to 'stop putting on airs and just talk like you naturally do. For God's sake, stop trying to sound like the Queen of England.' Harlow later gave Tracy the credit for making her a natural actor.

The parts Tracy was given did not improve and he became increasingly frustrated, having more and more rows with Sheehan. He found it particularly difficult to control his temper and there were several occasions when it got him into trouble. On the set of his next film, *She Wanted a Millionaire*, for example, he was angered by the fact that his co-star, Joan Bennett, had been given all the best lines. His comments that he felt more like an onlooker than an actor were printed in *The Hollywood Reporter*, as were stories about drunken brawls

Opposite: With Marguerite Churchill, who played Dorothy Stone in *Quick Millions*. Tracy is in unusually suave top-hatted mode as he romances the object of his affections.

Below: Spencer with Jean Harlow in *Goldie* (1931), in which he plays a sailor called Bill who has left a tattoo on a number of girls he has 'conquered'. One of these girls is Goldie, played by Jean Harlow. It was not a natural part for Tracy and contributed to his restlessness at Fox at this time.

Sto-35-21

he was involved in and an alleged romance with Bennett. The stories did not help the film, which received poor reviews.

Tracy went through a particularly bad time in 1932, when Louise was pregnant again. He worried that his second child might also be deaf, and was relieved when his daughter, Susie, was born perfectly normal. His dissatisfaction with the parts he was offered continued and he began to look for diversions from his frustrating career. He developed an interest in fine art, both collecting paintings and painting seascapes himself. Unfortunately, his other forms of release were not so tranquil. His drinking continued, and he formed part of what came to be known as either 'The Irishmen's Club' or 'The Boys' Club'. This was a group which met regularly in a number of different venues to socialize and to drink, and included Jimmy Cagney, Pat O'Brien, Ralph Bellamy, Frank McHugh, Frank Morgan and Lynne Overman. More sinister was Tracy's habit of disappearing for days on end, often while he was supposed to be filming. One of the places he would go to on these occasions was the St George Hotel in Brooklyn where, reputedly, he would sit in the bath drinking whisky. Nowadays Tracy would be recognized as an alcoholic and would be offered help. In those days he was supposed to fight his problem alone and it is to his credit that, for long stretches of time, he would resist the temptation to get drunk.

One of the better films Tracy appeared in at this time was *The Power and the Glory* (1933) in

Above: Tracy with his daughter Susie at the Tracys' ranch at Encino in the San Fernando Valley. He enjoyed escaping here from the studio.

Opposite: Joan Bennett, Spencer's co-star in *She Wanted a Millionaire* (1932); there were rumors of an affair between them.

Left: James Cagney was one of Tracy's fellow carousers in the informal drinking group nicknamed the Irishmen's Club or the Boys' Club. Here they are pictured at a open air barbecue organized by Pat O'Brien.

Right: Tracy with Loretta Young, with whom he had an affair that caused a temporary breach with Louise, in *A Man's Castle* (1933). The film tells the story of a down and out couple, Bill, played by Tracy and Trina, played by Young, during the Depression. Bill leaves Trina for a showgirl who can support him, but when he discovers that Trina is pregnant he returns to her and the couple marry.

Opposite: *The Power and Glory* (1933) was one of Tracy's first film successes. He is shown here, with Colleen Moore, in his role as the railroad tycoon who rises from poverty but is corrupted by power.

which he co-starred with Colleen Moore. It tells the story of Tom Garner (Tracy), a railway president, who devotes himself so much to his career that he does not notice that his son has fallen in love with his second wife. The story is told by his private secretary after Garner's funeral. The film was a hit with the critics, one of whom, William Troy in *The Nation*, wrote 'Spencer Tracy's railroad president is one of the fullest characterizations ever achieved on the screen.' As a result of the film's success, Tracy's contract was extended and he was given a large salary increase.

Unfortunately Tracy's struggles at Fox continued. He was involved in further scandal in 1933, when he had an affair with Loretta Young, his co-star in the film *A Man's Castle*. The gossip columnists went to town, reporting 'an exciting new romance between Spencer Tracy and Loretta Young.' Tracy denied the rumors but Young suggested that the couple

had been involved when she stated: 'Since Spencer Tracy and I are both Catholic and can never be married, we have agreed not to see each other again.' Unsurprisingly, Tracy's first separation from Louise was announced at this time. The separation lasted a year, during which Tracy was miserable. He eventually persuaded Louise to allow him to return to the family home.

After *The Power and the Glory* Tracy had hoped to be given better parts but he was disappointed. Throughout 1934 and 1935 he appeared in a series of mediocre films; the one exception was *The Show-Off*, a film version of George Kelly's Broadway hit play. It is interesting to note that Tracy made this film while he was on loan to Metro Goldwyn Mayer, the studio for which he was soon to make so many successful films. Back at the Fox studio, though, things were not going so well. Tracy argued almost constantly with Sheehan,

refusing to play several of the parts that were suggested to him. Sheehan asked him what he would be willing to do and he replied that he would be willing to work elsewhere. He was not allowed to go, however, until he had had one of his worst alcoholic bouts. He turned up on the set for *Dante's Inferno* roaring drunk, eventually falling asleep on a sofa that was a part of the set. To keep him safe, he was locked in the studio overnight by Sheehan. When Tracy woke up the next morning he was still angry and began destroying the sound stage. When he finished he had caused about $100,000 worth of damage. He went on to complete the film but he was then allowed to leave Fox – in fact he was sacked or, as Fox announced: 'Mr Tracy has asked for and received his release.' This was probably one of the best things that could have happened to Tracy for Metro Goldwyn Mayer decided to sign him up. At MGM he was to make some of his most famous films and was also destined to meet Hepburn.

Above: Tracy with Madge Evans in *The Show-Off* (1934), a comedy about the romance between Aubrey Piper, an adventurer played by Tracy and Amy Fisher, played by Evans.

Left: The singer and concert pianist Margarite McCrystal made her début as a trumpeter in *Dante's Inferno* (1935), Tracy's last film with MGM, in which he plays a ruthless and arrogant carnival owner who has a vision of hell induced by one of his own fairground attractions. The inferno sequence is a Hollywood classic.

Opposite: Spencer and Louise in relaxed mood together on board ship after Tracy had become a movie star.

Chapter 3
THE MOVIE STAR
1935-1941

IN the mid-1930s the Metro Goldwyn Mayer studio had on its books some of the most famous movie stars of the day, with a particularly strong group of female stars including Greta Garbo, Norma Shearer, Jean Harlow, Joan Crawford, Jeanette MacDonald and Myrna Loy. The male stars included Clark Gable, Robert Montgomery and William Powell. Louis B Mayer was originally reluctant to take Tracy on because of his troublesome

reputation but he was persuaded by Irving Thalberg, MGM's production manager, that Tracy, with his undeniable acting ability, would be an asset.

Tracy's first three films for MGM are not particularly memorable. *Murder Man* was shot very quickly in three weeks, before work began on *Riff Raff* in which he again appeared with Jean Harlow. The film received only mediocre reviews although, as usual, kind words were

Right: Tracy with Jean Harlow, Una Merkel and a young Mickey Rooney in *Riff Raff*. Tracy plays a fisherman, Dutch, married to Hattie (Harlow). He deserts Hattie after he is fired from his job but when Hattie finds out he needs money, she steals for him, is caught, and sent to prison. The couple are eventually reconciled.

found for Tracy. The *Hollywood Spectator* reported that 'Spencer Tracy is a bumptious, conceited ass throughout, giving a really splendid delineation of the character handed him.' He then co-starred with Myrna Loy in *Whipsaw*, a 'cops and robbers' film which, once again, received mediocre reviews but favorable comment for Tracy: 'Myrna Loy's charm and Tracy's skillful underplaying are assets that no picture can have and be bad.' (*Time*).

Tracy's next film was the one that launched him as a star. As usual with films that were going to be particularly successful for him, Tracy had grave doubts about the script of *San Francisco*. He was to play a priest, Father Mark, a friend of bar owner Blackie Norton, to be played by Clark Gable. The film tells the story of the love affair between Norton and Mary Blake, a singer, set against the backdrop of San Francisco in 1906, the year of the great earthquake. Tracy was concerned that it might be sacrilegious to play a priest and had to be persuaded to take the part by the director, W S Van Dyke II, who wanted Tracy's character to bring 'humanity' to the film. During production the two male actors, Tracy and Gable, developed a friendship that was to last for the three films they made together. They each

viewed themselves as men's men and the friendship was helped by Gable's profound respect for Tracy.

Production of *San Francisco* overlapped with Tracy's next film, *Fury*, but the two films were very different. *Fury* was directed by German director Fritz Lang, famous for such silent masterpieces as *Metropolis*. It is about a young man, Joe Wilson, played by Tracy, arrested as a suspect in a kidnapping while passing innocently through a small town. A lynch mob burns down the jail in which Wilson has been imprisoned and he is presumed dead but, in fact, manages to escape and hunt down his would-be killers and has them brought to trial. He appears at the trial and delivers a memorable speech about lynch law. Tracy did not get on as well with Lang as he did with Woody Van Dyke. Lang was a meticulous director who demanded that his actors spend hours on the set, often filming long into the evening. This angered Tracy, but anger was precisely the effect that Lang was aiming for. In the film Tracy had to play an exhausted man, emotionally and physically drained; Lang ensured that during the filming, Tracy was exactly that.

Fury and *San Francisco* were released within three weeks of each other and established

Above: Tracy with Clark Gable and Jeanette MacDonald in *San Francisco* (1936), the first film for which Tracy was nominated for the Academy Award for best actor. This caused some surprise, as Gable had top billing as saloon proprietor Blackie Norton.

Opposite: Tracy, as Father Mullin in *San Francisco*, surveying the destruction caused by the great earthquake which provides the climax to the movie.

Below: As Joe Wilson in *Fury* Spencer scored a second great success in 1936. Here he is seen at the beginning of the movie, innocently reading the local newspaper report of the kidnapping for which he is about to be arrested.

Spencer as a star. *Fury* became a hit with the art houses while *San Francisco* became a large box office success everywhere. In the *New York Times*, Frank S Nugent wrote of the latter film:

There must be special mention of another brilliant portrayal by Spencer Tracy, that of Father Mullin, the two-fisted chaplain of a Barbary Coast mission. Mr Tracy, late of *Fury*, is headed surely toward an award for the finest performance of the year.

The *Literary Review* said of *Fury* that 'Spencer Tracy brings lasting reality to the role of Joe.' For *San Francisco* it was Tracy rather than the top-billed Gable who was nominated as best actor in the Academy Awards, although he did not receive it. He was, however, given the Screen Writers' Guild award for the most distinguished performance of the month for two consecutive months, once for *Fury* and once for *San Francisco*.

The uproar on the set of Tracy's next film, *Libeled Lady*, confirmed his new star status; the set was over-run with reporters eager to document Tracy's activities. The cast of the film included another three of MGM's biggest stars, William Powell, Myrna Loy and Jean Harlow. Tracy enjoyed making the film, which was a farce and similar to many he had done on stage. The film did very well at the box office and was also received well by the critics:

Jean Harlow, Myrna Loy, William Powell and Spencer Tracy, . . . are just about as perfect a light comedy foursome as you will encounter anywhere between the rockbound coast of Maine and the sun-kissed shores of California.

Tracy did not take his newfound success for granted. He was now earning vast amounts of money but, unlike many of his contemporaries, he did not squander it. When he first moved to Hollywood he had persuaded his brother, Carroll, to move with him to manage his affairs. Carroll not only ran Tracy's finances but also looked after him during his drinking bouts. Tracy often slept at Carroll's house on Beverly Drive as he and Louise drifted further apart. He still turned to Louise for advice, however, and he asked her to read the script of his next film, *Captains Courageous*, hoping that she would advise him against doing it. Fortunately for Tracy, she advised him in favor.

Captains Courageous is an adaptation of Rudyard Kipling's classic novel of the same name. Tracy plays Manuel, a Portuguese fisherman who picks up Harvey Cheyne, the

Right: Tracy with Joan Crawford in *Mannequin*, which tells the story of the love affair between Jessie Cassidy, the wife of a small-time crook, played by Crawford, and shipping magnate John Hennessy, played by Tracy.

Below: *Libeled Lady* (1936) is a lively comedy about a libel suit taken by an heiress (Myrna Loy) against a newspaper edited by Haggerty, played by Tracy, and the efforts taken by him to have the case dropped, which include hiring a friend (William Powell) to compromise her. Here Tracy is seen with co-star Jean Harlow.

pampered but neglected son of a business tycoon, when he falls off a liner en route from America to Europe. Manuel cares for the boy with a kindness that he has never known before. When Manuel is killed during a race with another ship, Harvey is heartbroken and returns home to his father a changed character. Tracy was very anxious about taking on the part, later saying:

I worried that I'd look like a dope when they curled my hair for the part of Manuel and it didn't help any when Joan Crawford yelled from her car on the lot one day, 'Hey, look who's here. It's Harpo Marx.' Then I worried about learning a Portuguese accent. I had never done any accent before. But I researched how people from Portugal talk when they come to the U.S. of A., and I thought I had the problem licked. But then the studio brought in a real Portuguese American fisherman and I sat down in Victor Fleming's office to talk to him. I said, 'Now how would you say leetle fish?' and he said, 'I'd say little fish.'

In fact the filming of *Captains Courageous* went smoothly. Tracy had great respect for his fellow actors, Lionel Barrymore and Freddie Bartholomew, of whom he later said, 'Freddie was different, he was the only child actor I ever saw who was trying to be real instead of cute, and it's harder to be real.' The film also introduced Tracy to a new hobby, sailing. He had to learn how to row, fish, trawl and steer. As a result he bought a forty-foot ketch which he named the *Carrie B* after his mother.

Left: Spencer with his brother Carroll, whom he persuaded to become his business manager as soon as he moved to Hollywood.

Below: Tracy had nothing but praise for his co-star Freddie Bartholomew in *Captains Courageous* (1937), the first film for which he was awarded the Oscar for best actor. Freddie plays millionaire's son Harvey Cheyne, rescued from the Atlantic by a Portuguese fisherman (Tracy with curled hair), who is here seen teaching him to use a telescope.

Right: Louise Tracy receiving the Oscar for Best Actor in *Captains Courageous* on behalf of her husband, who was too ill to attend the ceremony. Also pictured are Luise Rainer, Best Actress in *The Good Earth*, and Frank Capra (far right).

Below: *Dr Jekyll and Mr Hyde* (1941), in which Spencer starred with Ingrid Bergman, was panned by *The New York Times* as 'not so much evil incarnate as ham rampant . . . more ludicrous than dreadful.'

The film was released to enthusiastic reviews. *Time* stated that:

So magnificent are its sweep and excitement, so harmonious its design that *Captains Courageous* ranks above most current cinematic efforts, offers its credentials for admission to the thin company of cinema immortals.

Tracy was again nominated for the 1937 Academy Award for Best Actor, but was unable to attend the Oscar ceremony because of ill health. He was in hospital for a hernia operation and so Louise attended in his place. When Tracy was named Best Actor she accepted the Oscar on his behalf, saying: 'I thank you for Spencer, Johnnie, Susie and myself and I want to tell all of you how much all of us appreciate it.'

Captains Courageous was followed by two relatively undistinguished films, *The Big City* and *Mannequin*, in which Spencer appeared with Joan Crawford, and then he starred in his second film with Clark Gable, *Test Pilot*. Spencer was at first reluctant to take the part for once again he would be playing second fiddle to Gable, but his part was given more importance and he set to work. The film certainly did him no harm, for it was well received by the critics and further increased Gable's respect for him:

The guy's good and there's nobody in this business who can touch him, so you're a fool to try. And don't fall for that humble stuff, either; the bastard knows it!

Tracy's next film was a far cry from the action and special effects of *Test Pilot*. Once again he was asked to play a priest, in the film *Boys' Town*; this time the real-life priest, Father Edward J Flanagan, who ran his famous institution for renegade young men in Nebraska on the assumption that 'there are no bad boys.' Tracy observed Father Flanagan in Omaha, getting to know him so that he could recreate this character as accurately as possible in the film. He later wrote: 'He's a great man – the greatest man I ever met.' His portrayal of

Above: Tracy with Clark Gable in the second of the three films they made together, *Test Pilot* (1938).

1027-54

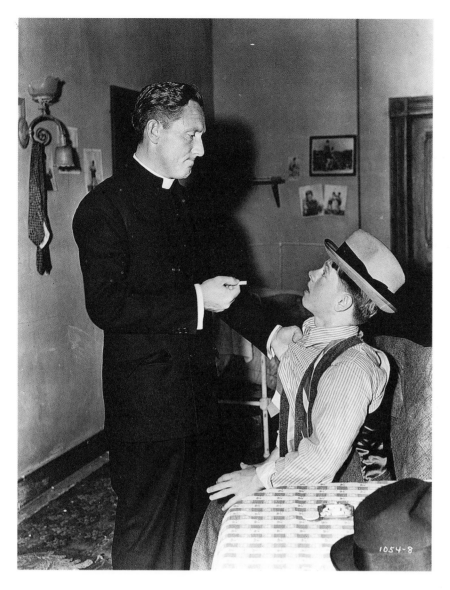

Father Flanagan was generally agreed to be his best performance ever when the film was released. Frank Nugent in the *New York Times* wrote that 'Spencer Tracy's performance of Father Flanagan is perfection itself.' For the second year in a row Tracy was awarded the Oscar for Best Actor. In his acceptance speech, he said that it really belonged to Father Flanagan and later gave the statuette to him, inscribed: 'To Father Edward J Flanagan whose great human qualities, timely simplicity, and inspiring courage were strong enough to shine through my humble effort.'

Tracy was now a huge star but he did not realize this until he traveled abroad; on a trip to London with Louise, he was mobbed by huge crowds desperate to catch a glimpse of their favorite movie star. Back in Hollywood his stardom caused more frustration, for now the studio kept him waiting while they decided on suitable film scripts in which to feature their money-making star. The films chosen did not rank with *Captains Courageous* or *Boys' Town*. *I Take this Woman*, with Hedy Lamarr, was ridiculed by the critics, and although *Northwest Passage* made money, Tracy himself considered it a failure.

As before when he had been frustrated with the poor quality of the films he was asked to do, Tracy sought consolation in the diversions Hollywood offered. He was seen around town with a number of different women, including Judy Garland and Olivia de Havilland. The spate of poor films continued, with only a couple of minor successes, such as *Edison the*

Above: Tracy, as the tough but sympathetic real-life priest Father Flanagan, holds a recalcitrant Mickey Rooney firmly by the collar in the much-acclaimed *Boys' Town* (1938). *Variety* described the movie as 'a production that should build goodwill for the whole industry.'

Right: With (from left) Mickey Rooney, Archbishop J. J. Cantwell, Father Flanagan and Louis B Mayer, pictured at an MGM lunch in honor of the real Father Flanagan, who founded the real Boys' Town in Nebraska.

Left: Henry Ford shows Spencer Thomas Edison's 'Corpse Reviver', built by the inventor to wake up employees who fell asleep on the job. In 1940 Spencer appeared in a film about the inventor's life, *Edison, the Man.*

Man and his last film with Clark Gable, *Boom Town*, and reached the nadir with *Dr Jekyll and Mr Hyde*, which was almost universally slated by the critics. He was in desperate need of a boost to his career, and was granted one in a way that changed not only his professional but also his personal life, for his next film was with Katharine Hepburn.

Left: Tracy with Bette Davis and Sir Cedric Hardwicke, after having been awarded his second Oscar for best actor in *Boys' Town.*

Chapter 4
KATHARINE HEPBURN
1942-1950

I<small>N</small> a particularly shrewd business move typical of her, Katharine Hepburn had arranged that should a film be made of *The Philadelphia Story*, the highly successful Broadway play in which she starred, be made she must play the female lead. In 1940, therefore, when MGM bought the film rights of the play, they had to include Hepburn. She had already made several films for RKO and had received an Oscar for her third film, *Morning Glory*. She had had several more successes, including *Little Women*, *Alice Adams*, *Stage Door*, *Bringing up Baby* and *Holiday*. In 1938, after several poor films, she returned to Broadway in

Right: After his pairing with Katharine Hepburn in *Woman of the Year* (1942), Spencer went on to make a number of successful movies with her, including *State of the Union* (1948), in which he played a presidential candidate and she played his estranged wife.

triumph in *The Philadelphia Story* and from Broadway she journeyed back to Hollywood, but this time to work for MGM rather than RKO. Hollywood had never known a female star like Hepburn. She flouted the conventional dress of the time, wearing slacks around town while other Hollywood women wore tailored suits and dresses. She was a highly intelligent young woman, a supporter of women's rights and a constant rebel against the Hollywood system.

This independent spirit had been encouraged and developed by her parents. She was born in Hartford, Connecticut to Dr Thomas Norval Hepburn, a surgeon urologist, and Katharine Martha Hepburn. They were both descended from early settlers in colonial America. Dr Hepburn was a liberal, an unusual political affiliation in conservative medical circles, and Mrs Hepburn was a campaigner for women's rights and birth control. Intellectual discussions in the Hepburn household were fierce and all the six children were encouraged to participate. Katharine's intellectual education was completed at Bryn Mawr, the elite women's college. After this she decided to go on the stage and began her acting career in stock. At the age of 21 she married Ludlow Ogden Smith but the marriage did not last, mainly because she found it difficult to live with another person. The couple, however, remained good friends.

After the huge success of *The Philadelphia Story*, in which she starred with Cary Grant and James Stewart, Hepburn was able to negotiate for a longterm MGM contract. Always meticulously careful about the films she appeared in, she began to look around for a

Left: Hepburn with Ruth Hussey, Jimmy Stewart and Cary Grant in *The Philadelphia Story* (1940). Hepburn had originally wanted Clark Gable and Tracy to play the two male lead roles, but Louis B Mayer refused to allow it, knowing that neither would accept roles that were secondary to Hepburn's.

Below: Tracy with Hepburn in *Woman of the Year* (1942), their first film together, which was closely based on their two characters.

Right: A still from *Woman of the Year*; Hepburn received her fourth Academy Award nomination for this film, and one critic said of Tracy and Hepburn: 'Between them they have enough charm to keep any ball rolling.'

Below: Together again in *Woman of the Year*. The critic in the *Baltimore Sun* wrote: 'Mr Tracy is an excellent foil for her [Hepburn] in this particular instance. His quiet, masculine stubborness and prosaic outlook on life is in striking contrast with her sparkle and brilliance.'

suitable script and found one written by two young writers, Ring Lardner Jr and Michael Kanin. The screenplay, called *Woman of the Year*, was based on a true story about the tempestuous relationship between Ring Lardner Jr's father and a famous political columnist, Dorothy Thompson. The story was re-worked so that the male character became a sportswriter, Sam Craig, writing for the same paper as the Thompson character, renamed Tess Harding. Hepburn loved the script and persuaded Mayer to take it on. She negotiated an enormous sum of money for the film, $211,000, which included $100,000 for the young, unknown writers and $10,000 for her agent. She also wanted Tracy to play Sam Craig. She had admired Tracy for some time, even writing to compliment him on his performance in the critically disastrous *Dr Jekyll and Mr Hyde*. It did not at first seem that Tracy would be able to appear in *Woman of the Year* for its schedule clashed with *The Yearling*, which he was already working on. Fortunately *The Yearling* had to be postponed because of a number of problems, including a plague of insects, during its filming in the Everglades, and so Tracy was free to appear in *Woman of the Year*.

There are a number of different stories relating to the famous first meeting between Tracy and Hepburn. Hepburn, who was only very slightly shorter than Tracy, is supposed to have said, 'I fear I may be too tall for you, Mr Tracy,' and he is reported to have replied, 'Don't worry, Miss Hepburn, I'll cut you down to size.' In fact it was probably the director Joe Mankiewicz, their mutual friend, who said that Tracy would cut her down to his size. The two actors soon lost their formality and before long were calling each other Spence and Kate. There was a closed set during the filming and so reporters had to keep their distance, but rumors did begin to leak out about an on-the-set romance between the two stars. The writer Michael Kanin, later said:

The magic between the two was evident on the sound stage. Maybe that's because the way we wrote the script, the characters of Sam Craig and Tess Harding were very much how we saw Spence and Kate in real life, the gruff, cantankerous but loving male and the wise accommodating female who ends up getting her own way.

The film, when it was released, was greeted very enthusiastically by everybody. Critics

Below: A still from *Woman of the Year*.

Right: The wedding scene in *Woman of the Year*. The two journalists' marriage does not go well at the first, as they discover the enormous differences between them. By the end of the film, however, an accommodation has been reached and the couple are reconciled to one another.

Below: *Keeper of the Flame* (1942), the couple's second film. After the success of *Woman of the Year* MGM quickly found another vehicle for them, a strongly anti-Fascist but not altogether successful piece, directed by George Cukor.

applauded it and *Time* recorded that:

Actors Hepburn and Tracy have a fine old time in *Woman of the Year*. They take turns playing straight for each other, act one superbly directed love scene, and succeed in turning several batches of cinematic corn into passable moonshine.

The audience also loved the film, revelling in the magic created by Tracy and Hepburn on screen. The on-screen romance was, of course, continued into the couple's personal lives, a romance that was to end only with Tracy's death. To many people the couple seemed ill-matched because they were so different. Perhaps Hepburn's attraction to Tracy can be explained in comments she made about their success in films together:

Certainly the ideal American man is Spencer. Sportsloving, a man's man. Stronglooking, a big sort of head, boar neck, and so forth. A man. And I think I represent a woman. I needle him, and I irritate him, and I try to get around him, yet if he put a big paw out, he could squash me.

The magic continued into the next film the couple made together, *The Keeper of the Flame*, directed by George Cukor. Again Tracy plays a journalist but this time the film has tragic overtones as the Tracy character investigates the death of a national hero. In the process he falls in love with the hero's widow, played by Hepburn, and persuades her to reveal her husband's guilty secret.

The Tracy separation was not widely known and it was generally believed that they still lived together. This idea was underlined by Tracy's support of the John Tracy Clinic for the deaf that Louise founded in 1942. She had worked to teach John to lipread and to talk and given many speeches about the problems of rearing deaf children. When she was offered the use of a dilapidated building on the campus of the University of Southern California, she accepted readily. The clinic grew rapidly and was incorporated in 1943 with Tracy as one of its directors. It continued to expand, moved into a more spacious custom-made building, and still exists today, famous for its work with deaf children. In its early days Tracy donated huge sums of money to it, arranging for the premieres of his films to be charity benefits. Louise became a world expert in her field; in the dedication ceremony of the clinic, Tracy said:

Below: In *Keeper of the Flame* Tracy plays a journalist who suspects that Hepburn, as the widow of a national hero, played some part in her husband's death. She is in fact trying to protect his reputation by concealing the truth about his political activities.

Right: Louise Tracy (left) explaining how the vocal chords are used. This photograph was taken at the opening session of the 52nd meeting of the American Academy of Ophthalmology and Otolaryngology, one of the many professional bodies Louise addressed about her work at the John Tracy Clinic for the Deaf.

Below: Tracy with his son John. Louise had spent years teaching John to lip read. Tracy often expressed admiration for his wife's patience with their son, admitting that he soon became frustrated when attempting to teach him.

You honor me because I am a movie actor, a star in Hollywood terms. Well, there's nothing I've ever done that can match what Louise has done for deaf children and their parents.

As this quotation shows, Tracy remained highly supportive of Louise and his children. Jessie Blakiston, a board member of the clinic for thirty years, recalled:

He was always there when we needed him, if he was available. I can say the same about his attitude toward his children. I don't think there was a single parent's affair at Susie's Westlake school that he didn't attend, big movie star or not.

By 1942 Tracy had moved out permanently from the Encino ranch. He now lived in a suite at the Beverly Hills Hotel, where he and Hepburn would have breakfast every morning after she had played tennis on the hotel's courts, but his loyalty to his family remained constant even when his career started to deteriorate. During the war years patriotic films depicting young soldiers, sailors and airmen were fashionable. Tracy, although only in his early forties, looked older; he was suffering from kidney and bladder problems, probably caused by alcohol. The lines on his face had deepened further and already his hair was turning gray, and MGM found it difficult to find appropriate films for him. The first one they found for him was *A Guy Named Joe*, about the ghost of a flying ace (Tracy), who comes back to influence the lives of those he left behind, including his former sweetheart, played by Irene Dunne. Possibly because Hepburn was in New York, appearing on Broadway in the play *Without Love*, Tracy was particulary bad-tempered during the filming of *A Guy Named Joe*, making Irene Dunne's life very difficult with his teasing. He also, however, demonstrated

Left: Tracy with Van Johnson in *A Guy Named Joe* (1943), one of the films found for him by MGM during the Second World War to show him patriotically in uniform. He plays a dead flying ace who returns to supervise his girlfriend's new romance.

Below: Tracy with Jessica Tandy and Hume Cronyn in *The Seventh Cross* (1944), set in Nazi Germany in 1936. Tracy plays George Heisler, who escapes with six others from a concentration camp and is the only one not to be recaptured and crucified by the Nazis.

the generosity of his nature, as well as its taciturnity, during the shooting of this film. The part of the young flyer with whom Irene Dunne's character falls in love was played by an actor named Van Johnson. During the production of the film Johnson had a bad motorcycle accident, from which it took him a long time to recover, and the studio started to look for a replacement for him. When Tracy discovered this, he declared that if Johnson went he would have to go too; Johnson's film career was saved and he went on to star in *Two Girls and a Sailor*, becoming the idol of American schoolgirls. *A Guy Named Joe* was not a huge success, and nor were Tracy's other films of this time, *The Seventh Cross* and *Thirty Seconds over Tokyo*. This latter film, in which Tracy did not have a large part, became a popular war picture but Tracy was dissatisfied with it. MGM tried to revive his interest in his work by buying the film rights of *Without Love*, the play Katharine Hepburn was appearing in on Broadway. The film was not one of the more successful of the Tracy/Hepburn films, however, although it did receive reasonable reviews, with James Agee in *The Nation* writing that 'Katharine Hepburn and Spencer Tracy are exactly right for their jobs.'

Perhaps in an attempt to sharpen his acting skills, Tracy returned to Broadway in 1945 to appear in a play by Robert Emmett Sherwood called *The Rugged Path*. Katharine Hepburn regularly returned to Broadway to hone her acting skills and she may have persuaded Tracy to do likewise. Robert Sherwood had been a celebrated playwright before the war but had given up writing plays during the conflict to become an adviser and speechwriter for President Roosevelt. Tracy was impressed by *The Rugged Path*, but had not acted in a play for over fifteen years and was extremely anxious about appearing before a live audience again. Unfortunately the critics did not agree with his assessment of the play, and it also received poor reviews in Washington during its two-week run there. Tracy was depressed by the critics' reaction but Hepburn managed to boost his morale before the play moved to Boston. Here too, the reviews were critical, although they praised Tracy's acting, and at this point Tracy threatened to leave. He was persuaded to stay, but when the play reached Broadway it was panned by the critics, although once again they were kind to Tracy. He contrived to stay until his son John had seen it but once John had flown in and

Opposite: With Hepburn in *Without Love* (1945), in which Tracy plays scientist Pat Jamieson, who marries Jamie Rowan, played by Hepburn, for convenience because he needs a home and an assistant. Gradually the marriage of convenience turns into a true marriage as the couple fall in love.

Below: Another still from *Without Love*. Hepburn had previously appeared in the stage version of the story, which was much less successful than the film. Many felt the play would have fared better had Tracy appeared in it.

1340-94

Opposite: Tracy and Hepburn in *The Sea of Grass* (1947) in which they played a cattle tycoon and his wife. He resists the arrival of homesteaders on his grazing ranges but loses a critical legal judgment. His wife then leaves him for his bitterest enemy; the film is considered to be one of the least effective of the Tracy/Hepburn films.

Below: Tracy during the filming of *Cass Timberlane* (1947), which co-starred Lana Turner as the working-class girl who marries Judge Timberlane, played by Tracy. At first things are difficult but all ends happily.

watched his father on stage, Tracy gave up his role. He returned to Hollywood, never to appear in a play again.

In Hollywood he tried to restore his confidence by making another film with Hepburn. Unfortunately, *Sea of Grass* was not one of their more successful films; it was directed by Elia Kazan, who was something of a Method director and failed to get on with Tracy, whose famous theory of acting was 'learn your lines and don't bump into the furniture.' Despite the film's title the cast and crew did not see one blade of grass during its production, the entire film being shot in the studio rather than on location. The reviews were terrible and it is considered the least successful of the couple's films. Tracy hoped his next film, *Cass Timberlane* in which he co-starred with Lana Turner, would restore morale and it was indeed a money-maker, but it was less successful dramatically.

In 1948 he once again tried his fortunes with a film co-starring Hepburn. *State of the Union* was originally supposed to have co-starred Claudette Colbert but she had to pull out at the last moment, and Hepburn stepped in to take Colbert's part. Tracy and Hepburn play

respectively a presidential candidate and his estranged wife, who makes the politician realize that he has sold out his principles and persuades him to withdraw from the presidential campaign. The film was a success both at the box office and with the critics. Howard Barnes in the *New York Herald Tribune* wrote:

With [Tracy's] forthright acting and his knowledge of the nuances which make a screen scene click, he brings a satirical and very human account of political skullduggery into sharp focus. Aiding and abetting him no end is Katharine Hepburn.

The political subject matter of the film was very appropriate for the time. The House Un-American Activities Committee was investigating many prominent Hollywood people, including Katharine Hepburn. She stood up to the Committee in her usual strong and defiant manner, whereas Tracy did not as publicly criticize the 'red scare' campaign, believing that actors should not get involved with politics. Any political message they wanted to make could be conveyed in films such as *State of the Union*.

The next Tracy/Hepburn film was even more successful, but before making *Adam's Rib*

Left: Publicity poster for *Dr Jekyll and Mr Hyde* (1941), a film for which, unusually, Tracy's performance was condemned by the critics. Katharine Hepburn, however, admired Tracy's acting in the film and wrote to tell him so. It was the beginning of her respect for him.

Below and opposite: Publicity posters for *Woman of the Year* and *Adam's Rib.*

in 1949, Tracy had to undergo the humiliation of *Edward My Son*, an unsuccessful film transcription of a play about a rich, unscrupulous man's belated regret for his treatment of his son. Tracy's co-star in the film was Deborah Kerr, who fared much better for she was a natural in a film based on the British class system, whereas Tracy's American accent struck a discordant note in the film and his performance was slated by the critics. He was relieved to start work on *Adam's Rib*, a screenplay written specifically for him and Hepburn by Garson Kanin and his wife, Ruth Gordon. It is about a married couple, both successful lawyers, who find themselves on opposite sides of the courtroom in a case about a woman's right to shoot her unfaithful husband. It was a huge success and is probably the best loved of all the Tracy/Hepburn films. Bosley Crowther in the *New York Times* wrote that their:

Perfect compatibility in comic capers is delightful to see. A line thrown away, a lifted eyebrow, a smile or a sharp, resounding slap on a tender part of the anatomy is as natural as breathing to them. Plainly, they took great pleasure in playing this rambustious spoof.

The money the film made was desperately needed by MGM, which was in financial troubles. 1949 was the first year of mass-marketed home television sets and, as a result, the movie-going audience dwindled. The lure of the televison, however, did not keep the audience away from the cinemas when they could see a classic Tracy/Hepburn vehicle such as *Adam's Rib*.

Above and left: Tracy and Hepburn in *Adam's Rib* (1949), one of the most successful of the couple's films. The writers Garson and Ruth Kanin modeled the characters of the screen couple played by Tracy and Hepburn on the actors themselves, with whom they were close friends.

Opposite: A typical scene from *Adam's Rib* as the couple have an argument. Both lawyers, they are on opposite sides in a court case that turns on women's rights issues, and tensions overflow at home.

Chapter 5
THE FATHER FIGURE
1950-1958

TRACY was now the 'grand old man' of Hollywood. Aged 50, his hair was completely gray and, at 190 pounds, his figure was distinctly portly. He and Clark Gable had been superseded by a new set of young male stars, who included Gene Kelly and Frank Sinatra. Tracy's interests became more those of a middle-aged man; he sought his own company more often, spending his time reading and listening to classical music (Brahms was a particular favorite). MGM had to look around for appropriate films for their ageing star, and found one in a screenplay by Frances Goodrich and Albert Hacket called *Father of the Bride*, about a lawyer, Stanley T Banks, coping with the trials and tribulations of preparing for his daughter's wedding. Tracy's screen wife was to be played by Joan

Right: A publicity poster for *A Guy Named Joe*, which cast Spencer as a ghostly flying ace, justifying putting him into uniform.

Spencer TRACY
Irene DUNNE
IN
A GUY NAMED Joe

"What are you trying to do — win this war single-handed?"

Bennett and their daughter by an eighteen-year-old Elizabeth Taylor. Tracy thought it was incredible that he could have produced a daughter as beautiful as Elizabeth Taylor, but she did in fact bear a likeness to Joan Bennett. He confessed that Taylor's beauty always gave him a start at the beginning of each day's shooting. Tracy's transition from romantic lead to character actor was confirmed by the critics when the film was released, who wrote of his comeback, when he had hardly been away. *Newsweek* said: 'Spencer Tracy hilariously sparks *Father of the Bride* with one of his surest comedy performances.'

It is interesting that Tracy was nominated for the Oscar for Best Actor for the first time in twelve years for *Father of the Bride*. He was never nominated for any of the films he made in partnership with Katharine Hepburn; the success of those films was obviously due to the brilliant acting by both halves of the partnership. Although *Father of the Bride* is only a slight film dramatically it carved the way for the great character parts Tracy was to play in the last years of his life.

After making *Father of the Bride* Tracy slipped into one of the depressions that he suffered throughout his life, this time caused by a number of different factors. Katharine Hepburn was away for a long time on location for *The African Queen*; the 'red scare' had hit Hollywood and many had their careers ruined overnight; and in 1951 Louis B Mayer lost his job at MGM, not because of the red scare but because of a boardroom re-shuffle. Dore Schary stayed on but the golden era when MGM produced the most successful films in the world was over; and instead it now produced some of the world's worst films, including such flops as *Never Let Me Go* with Clark Gable and *Soldiers Three* with Stewart Granger. Tracy's next two films did not help the studio's reputation. *Father's Little Dividend*, a sequel to *Father of the Bride*, did not do nearly as well as the first film, but at least it was better than *The People Against O'Hara*, in which Tracy as an alcoholic lawyer starred with his old friend, Pat O'Brien.

Tracy's depression lifted on Katharine Hepburn's return from Africa and the arrival of a script by the Kanins for another Hepburn and Tracy film, *Pat and Mike*. The film was directed by Cukor, and the combination of so much talent and so much experience was unbeatable. Garson Kanin later described the two stars reading through the screenplay:

Above: With Elizabeth Taylor in *Father of the Bride* (1950), the film that marked the change from romantic to character roles for Tracy.

Spencer sat in a corner of the room, his eyeglasses perched upon his nose. He began to read, to act – the man with whom we had dined a few minutes earlier was no longer there. Instead we were confronted by Mike – a personality far more real and complex than the one we had imagined – with a way of breathing, thinking, smoking, coughing, speaking and munching peanuts . . . I saw the art of acting that night, plain.

The film was a comedy about a sports promoter called Mike, played by Tracy, and his relationship with a sports teacher turned golf champion, Pat, played by Hepburn. The film was another success for the couple.

Unfortunately, Tracy's next movie did less well. *The Plymouth Adventure* was a technicolor film like *Northwest Passage*, and like *Northwest Passage* it was a flop; it suffered from a terrible script to which even Tracy could not bring life. He began to look around for a suitable screenplay for himself, as MGM seemed unable to find one for him, and thought he had found it in *The Mountain* by Henri Troyat, a screenplay about the rescue of the survivors from a plane crash. MGM decided that it was too expensive to make, however, and this was the beginning of the end of Tracy's career at MGM. Several stars were now working freelance, having freed themselves of their studio contracts, and some of these were earning enormous sums of money as a result; they arranged to be paid a percentage of the profits made on a film, rather than a salary. It was a risk, but the appeal to Tracy of this type of arrangement was not only the possibility of

Above: Tracy with his screen grandson in *Father's Little Dividend* (1950), the sequel to *Father of the Bride*, which tells the story of Stanley Banks's reaction to the arrival of his first grandchild.

Right: In *Pat and Mike* (1952), another successful film for the Tracy/Hepburn team, he plays a sports promoter who determines to make her a star. It was the last film Hepburn made while under contract to MGM.

Opposite: Tracy with Gene Tierney in *Plymouth Adventure* (1952), a well-meaning but dull retelling of the *Mayflower* story.

MGM PRESENTS **SPENCER TRACY**

KATHARINE HEPBURN

Together again — and it's no fib, Their funniest hit since "Adam's Rib"

PAT AND MIKE

CO STARRING **ALDO RAY**

WITH **WILLIAM CHING**

WRITTEN BY RUTH GORDON AND GARSON KANIN · DIRECTED BY GEORGE CUKOR · PRODUCED BY LAWRENCE WEINGARTEN AN M·G·M PICTURE

Above: This publicity poster for *Pat and Mike* features a curvaceous Katharine Hepburn in shorts.

higher financial reward but also the greater choice and control of the films he would have. He did not at this stage decide to cut himself off completely from his MGM contract, instead negotiating a deal that enabled him to make occasional films for other studios while still being paid a reduced salary by MGM. He would only be obliged to make one film a year for MGM instead of two and as he said: 'The company doesn't make two good pictures a year any more. I only want to be in the good one.'

His one film for MGM in 1953 was *The Actress* with Jean Simmons, a good film but not a great one. Again he played the father figure, a character he had now perfected. The following year he made one film only, a western called *Broken Lance* for Twentieth Century Fox, another moderately successful movie, about the relationship between a self-made cattle baron, Matt Devereux, and his sons, whom he treats as ranch hands. It was criticized as being rather cliché-ridden but once again Tracy's role was received favorably. *Newsweek* reported that he acted 'with an elder statesman's freedom and authority.'

Tracy returned to make his last film for MGM in 1955, called *Bad Day at Black Rock*. In 1953, when Tracy first read the short story upon which the film was based, he thought it was terrible and refused to do it but after he had read the second version of the screenplay, written by Millard Kaufman, he agreed at once. The film is set in a small hamlet in the Californian desert in which a World War Two officer, played by Tracy, arrives to present a posthumous medal to the Japanese father of one of his soldiers. He is received with intense hostility by the men of the town and he eventually deduces that they have killed the Japanese man. The audience does not at first know why Tracy has arrived in the town, which creates an atmosphere of suspense that pervades the whole film. The exterior scenes were shot on location in a small town called Lone Pine, on the edge of Death Valley, California. Filming took place during the swelteringly hot summer months but, contrary to many reports, Tracy did not react to the discomfort of his surroundings by escaping on numerous drinking binges; he said that knowing he was making a good film made the physical punishment worthwhile. Kaufman, who had written a brilliant script, praised Tracy for bringing even more conviction to his character:

. . . Film is a medium of reaction. Spence knew this. He was better at responding and reacting than anyone I've ever seen work . . . For example, he always scratched his nose when he was thinking in real life. He did that, too, when he was acting . . . both [Clark Gable and Tracy] conveyed their inner thoughts with reactions, which are hard as hell to write into a script.

The cast for the film was impressive, including Robert Ryan, Anne Francis, Ernest Borgnine, Dean Jagger, Walter Brennan and Lee Marvin. When the film was released they were all praised for giving magnificent performances. The novelist John O'Hara wrote:

As to the acting, well, at least a gold cigarette case to everyone in the cast. Everyone, from Spencer Tracy on. I'm sure Spencer Tracy had a gold cigarette case, but he ought to get a special one for his performance and so ought the other actors.

He also said that the film was 'one of the finest motion pictures ever made.' Once again Tracy was nominated for the Academy Award for best actor although his fellow actor in *Bad Day*, Ernest Borgnine, was awarded the Oscar for his performance in *Marty*. It was said at the time that if Tracy had fulfilled his threat to retire he would have received the Oscar.

Right: Tracy on horseback in *Broken Lance* (1954), the story of an autocratic cattle baron who causes dissension between his sons.

Below: Tracy comes the heavy in *Broken Lance* with William Conrad, Richard Widmark and Earl Holliman.

Although *Bad Day at Black Rock* was the last film Tracy completed for MGM, it was not the last one he began to make for the studio. This was *Tribute to a Bad Man*, a western which was to be filmed in the Rockies, near Montrose in Colorado. Tracy arrived on the set a week late with no explanation to the director, Robert Wise. After one day on set, he disappeared for another week. When he returned, again with no explanation, he complained about the effects of the high altitude at which the set was located. Wise brought in Howard Strickling, the studio publicity chief and a vice president, to try to bring about a peace settlement, but the attempt was useless; Wise complained to Sam Zimbalist at MGM, who agreed to drop Tracy from the film. After 20 years with MGM as one of its greatest stars, having helped to establish the studio as one of the most successful film-making organizations in the world, Tracy had been fired.

Although Tracy had wanted to leave MGM, this was not the way he wanted to go; he was distraught at the news that he had been sacked. The story did not appear in the press; MGM continued to spread the news that Tracy was on location and gave out press releases detailing his activities, such as judging plays in local schools and visiting a ranch to buy horses. Then there was a supposed break in filming attributed to technical problems and, by the time James Cagney took Tracy's part in the film, the press had forgotten that he had originally been in it. The few reporters who did

Above: Tracy with Walter Brennan in a scene from *Bad Day at Black Rock* (1955), the last film he completed with MGM. Brennan played Doc Velie, Black Rock's mortician and veterinary surgeon.

Left: With Mary Adam, William Demarest, Claire Trevor, E G Marshall, Jim Hayward and Richard Garrick in *The Mountain* (1956), which Spencer made as a freelance.

Opposite: A bearded Tracy in deep discussion with director Fred Zinnemann, on location during the making of *The Old Man and the Sea* (1958), based on Hemingway's story of an old fisherman's dream of hooking a great fish. With its minimal action and long monologues, it did not transfer well to the screen.

Above: With John Ericsson, who played a sycophantic hotel clerk in *Bad Day at Black Rock.*

pick up the fact that Tracy had been fired kept the story to themselves. When Gable had left the studios over money matters, the story had been very different: they had publicized the affair widely. This respect accorded Tracy by the press is now famous, and is the reason why his affair with Katharine Hepburn was kept secret for so many years.

Now that he had been forced to leave MGM, Tracy was free to make *The Mountain*, the film MGM had considered too expensive to make. Ironically, it was filmed in the French Alps at twelve thousand feet, a much higher altitude than he had complained about on location for *Tribute to a Bad Man*. His co-star in this film was Robert Wagner who rather improbably, at the age of 26, played Tracy's brother. Tracy had developed a liking for Wagner on *Broken Lance* and asked for him in *The Mountain*. He treated Wagner like a son, spending days with him in Paris, taking him around art galleries and introducing him to his distinguished friends there. Wagner later commented on the power of Tracy's acting:

Spence didn't analyse. He came to work so very well prepared and then figured out how to use the props, the set, even me, to enrich his performance . . . He looked like he was doing nothing, but he had tremendous power, tremendous power. I often wondered why there has never been a Tracy cult, like there's a Humphrey Bogart cult. Maybe it's because Spence was so good, he made it look too easy.

The Mountain was not well received by either the public or the critics, with many people commenting on the improbability of Tracy having a brother 30 years younger than him.

Unfortunately his next two ventures did not fare well either. In an attempt to regain some of his old popularity Tracy made another film, *Desk Set*, with Katharine Hepburn in 1957, but it did not match the success of the couple's other movies. Tracy was finding it difficult to find good scripts for himself, but thought he had done so when he agreed to play the Old Man in an adaptation of Ernest Hemingway's *The Old Man and the Sea*. The original director, Fred Zinnemann, gave up halfway through, after constant arguments with Tracy, and there was another crisis after Tracy and Hemingway got drunk and caused $150,000 worth of damage in a bar in Havana. Unsurprisingly after all these troubles, the film was an enormous flop. *Time*'s review said reproachfully: 'Tracy usually plays himself with a difference. This time he plays himself with indifference.'

Deeply depressed by the problems with *The Old Man and the Sea*, Tracy rushed into his next project, *The Last Hurrah* with his old friend Pat O'Brien. This film, about the last campaign of a dying Irish politician in New England, was a success and the critics suggested that his performance deserved an Academy Award; ironically, however, it was for his performance in *The Old Man and the Sea* that he was Oscar nominated in 1958.

Right and below: Tracy and Hepburn in *Desk Set* (1957). Hepburn plays Bunny, who runs a reference and research department for a television network, and Tracy is Richard, an efficiency expert who is sent to assess Bunny's office for the introduction of an electronic brain to take over some of the routine work.

Chapter 6
THE STANLEY KRAMER
FILMS *1959-1967*

Below: A particularly poignant photograph of Spencer and Kate. In the last decade of his life, she made very few films and spent all her spare time with him.

AFTER *The Last Hurrah* Tracy did not make another film for a year, meanwhile living in seclusion in a small rented house on George Cukor's property on the border of Beverly Hills. Katharine Hepburn did not work during this year either, spending her time looking after the increasingly ill Tracy. He had been suffering for many years from problems associated with his drinking. Many people have commented that Tracy would not have lived as long as he did without Hepburn. She controled his drinking to a certain extent, distracting him when he appeared to be about to go on another bender. During the filming of *The Mountain*, for example, when she could not be with him, she arranged for her secretary to be on location with him to keep an eye on him. Their romance was Hollywood's best kept secret for over 20 years; amazingly the gossip columnists of the time did not write about the couple, although they were producing almost libelous stories about the other movie stars of the time. Tracy and Hepburn were protected for a number of reasons. While Tracy had been working at MGM, the studio's policy had been to ignore the romance; it had issued publicity releases that Tracy was happily married to Louise and lived at home. Hepburn and Tracy did not live a public life in Hollywood, Hepburn in particular hating the Hollywood scene. They preferred to spend their time walking in the Hollywood hills, relaxing in New England or touring Europe.

The reasons why they never married have been well documented. Tracy was a devout Catholic and would never attempt to divorce Louise. Indeed, it is highly unlikely that Hepburn would have agreed to marry him even if he had believed in divorce. She once said, 'I don't believe in marriage. It isn't a natural institution – if it were, why sign a contract for it?'

Their relationship was one of opposites, each of them possessing qualities that complemented the other's. Hepburn was given to sudden enthusiasms, interested in the arts and the life of the mind, whereas Tracy's temperament was more steady and he was interested in more down-to-earth pursuits such as sport. The pair introduced each other to worlds they had not experienced before and thereby enriched each other's lives. Hepburn has made several comments on the relationships they portrayed in their films that might just as easily apply to their real relationship:

The woman is always pretty sharp. She needles the man, a little like a mosquito. Then he slowly puts out his big paw and slaps the lady down . . . In the end he's always the boss of the situation, but he's challenged by her.

The couple's deep feelings for each other were obvious to everybody who worked with them. Garson Kanin said, 'Here were two who brought out the best in everyone and in each other, personally and professionally.'

By 1960, Tracy and Hepburn had settled down to their quiet life in the house in Beverly Hills and it was commonly accepted that Tracy had retired. Stanley Kramer, however, had other plans for Tracy than a quiet retirement. Kramer had been an assistant film director at MGM just after the Second World War and, studying Tracy's pictures in the cutting room, he recognized his greatness. By 1960 Kramer had established his own reputation as a director with such films as *The Wild One*, *The Pride and the Passion* with Cary Grant and Frank Sinatra and *The Defiant Ones* with Tony Curtis and Sidney Poitier; and was now planning a film, *Inherit the Wind*, based on the Scopes 'monkey trial' in Tennessee in 1925, in which a teacher was taken to court for teaching Darwin's theory of evolution, which was contrary to the state law. The trial was a classic confrontation between the lawyer Clarence Darrow and an ex-presidential candidate, William Jennings Bryan. Kramer wanted Tracy to play Darrow (called Drummond in the film) who was on the side of evolution:

From the very beginning, I knew there was only one actor in the world to play the Clarence Darrow character – and that was Spencer Tracy. I called him and we had a meeting. He played it close to the vest, didn't give me too much warmth. He said, 'I

Below: Tracy with Gene Kelly, Donna Anderson and Dick York in *Inherit the Wind* (1960), the first film he made with Kramer. It was based on a real-life court case about the right to teach the theory of evolution.

might as well do it. Nobody else wants me. It would be better than just sitting home.'

Kramer chose Tracy's old friend Fredric March to play Brady Drummond's sparring partner in the courtroom and, in yet another unusual casting idea, Gene Kelly for the role of the reporter.

At first production of the film did not go smoothly. On the first day's shooting, Kramer asked Tracy to repeat a line that was unintelligible because Tracy had mumbled. Tracy is said to have replied:

Mr Kramer, it has taken me 30 years to speak lines. If you or a theater arts major from UCLA wants to do this speech, I am quite willing to step aside.

The crisis was soon averted by Kramer calmly asking for another take and Tracy agreeing. Having thus established the ground rules, Tracy developed a particularly close relationship with Kramer; making the film was very enjoyable for Tracy and, indeed, for everybody else on the set. Although officially the set was closed, it was packed every day by as many as could manage it, watching Tracy and Fredric March produce the performances of their lifetimes. Each take by the two veteran actors was greeted by loud applause. When the film was released, late in 1960, it was a huge critical success and two months later Tracy was nominated for his seventh Academy Award. Tracy was full of praise for Kramer:

Left: Stanley Kramer with the special Oscar he was awarded in 1961, the Irving Thalberg Award, for 'consistently high quality in film-making.'

Opposite: Tracy listens wryly to his adversary, here called Matthew Harrison Brady and played by Fredric March, in one of the trial scenes from *Inherit the Wind*.

Below: In another courtroom scene in *Judgment at Nuremberg* (1961). This time, however, Spencer is playing a stern-faced judge rather than a witty and entertaining lawyer.

Stanley is a lot like Irving Thalberg, very smart and really in love with the movie business, only warmer than Thalberg and not so much driven by money.

He also told Kramer that he would do any film directed by him. His next film, *The Devil at*

Four O'Clock with Frank Sinatra, was not directed by Kramer and was a failure. He was happy to return to a Stanley Kramer film and a script he said was 'the best I've read in years.' This was *Judgment at Nuremberg*, based on a television play about the war crimes trials held in Germany by the Allies after the Second World War. The writer had tried without success to persuade the film studios to make it into a film; all had been reluctant to make a film about the massacre of six million Jews in the Nazi concentration camps. Once Tracy had found out about it, however, he said that he would appear in the film if it was directed by Kramer.

With Tracy and Kramer both committed, the project soon gained the backing it needed. The rest of the cast was impressive, including Marlene Dietrich, Burt Lancaster, Maximillian Schell, Robert Widmark and, in cameo parts, Judy Garland and Montgomery Clift.

As was usual now, Katharine Hepburn was on the set every day presiding over Tracy, ensuring he took his medicines and drank his milk and acting as a nurse companion to him. Tracy, in his turn, kept an eye on one of his fellow actors, Montgomery Clift, who was suffering terribly from the ravages of alcoholism. During the filming of Clift's one long sequence he started to falter, unable to remember his lines. Tracy, as Kramer recalled, 'grabbed Monty's shoulders and told him he was the greatest young actor of his generation, and to look into his eyes and play to him, to hell with the lines.' In the end, Clift received an Academy Award nomination for his part in *Judgment at Nuremberg*, due largely to Tracy's support.

In the film Tracy plays a retired judge from New England who presided at the war crimes trial of four former Nazi judges. The film broke new ground in focusing on the Holocaust and attracted much attention when it was released. Willy Brandt, then Mayor of West Berlin, said at its world premiere in that city:

The film *Judgment at Nuremberg*, which will raise a great many questions, is ensuring by its world premiere in Berlin that its own importance, as well as that of Berlin as a center of spiritual conflict, is heavily underlined.

Much discussion took place about the suitability of the subject matter for film, but praise for all the principal actors concerned was universal. Larry Tubelle in *Daily Variety* wrote:

As the presiding judge, Tracy delivers a performance of great intelligence and intuition. He creates a gentle but towering figure, compassionate but realistic, warm but objective – a person of unusual insight and eloquence, but also a plain, simple human being demandingly sandwiched between politics and justice.

During the filming of *Judgment at Nuremberg* Kramer made many allowances for Tracy's deteriorating health. He was suffering from problems with his kidneys, bladder and liver and was easily tired. After he had finished the film, Tracy announced that he would not make any more films, except that is for the 'good ones that Stanley does.' The next film 'Stanley did' was very different from the other Kramer films Tracy had appeared in. *It's a Mad Mad Mad Mad World* starred an impressive group of comedians including, among others, Milton Berle, Sid Caesar, Buddy Hacket, Ethel Merman, Mickey Rooney, Dick Shawn and Phil Silvers. Tracy enjoyed making the film; being surrounded by so many comedians ensured that he was constantly entertained. It was shot mainly on location in Palm Springs, where it was very hot, and so Kramer provided a large air-conditioned truck where the cast congregated to get away from the heat. The comedians spent their spare time amusing Tracy, making jokes for his benefit. The film was a success and remains a cult movie to this day. The plot focuses on a group of crooks intent on finding the stored fortune hidden by the late Smiler Grogan. As they search for the fortune, the crooks are unaware that they are being watched by the police, headed by Captain Culpeper, played by Tracy. Once they have been put in jail after finding the money, Culpeper himself absconds with the money, only to lose it during a wild chase.

After making this, his third Kramer film, Tracy's health deteriorated sharply. He was rushed to hospital in 1963 with pulmonary edema and then in 1965 he had to have a prostatectomy. After this operation complications developed, and for several days he was in a critical condition. Louise Tracy and Katharine Hepburn took it in turns to sit by his bedside. When he recovered Tracy went into almost total seclusion. He occasionally visited Louise in her house in Beverly Hills and could sometimes be seen out on walks with Katharine Hepburn. Hepburn did not make a single film between 1962 and 1967, as she devoted herself to caring for Tracy, and the reason she did finally return to the screen was so that she could continue caring for him. Kramer had approached both Tracy and Hepburn to appear in his film *Guess Who's Coming to Dinner*.

Below: Tracy and Elizabeth Ashley on the set of *Ship of Fools* (1965), a Kramer film in which he did not star.

Right and below: With Hepburn, Sidney Poitier and Katharine Houghton (Hepburn's niece) in *Guess Who's Coming to Dinner* (1967). The film appealed to Hepburn and Tracy because of its advocacy of racial tolerance and understanding, although the prospective bridegroom was so outstandingly eligible that even at the time some wondered whether the bride was worthy of him, rather than the other way round.

Tracy's health had not improved but he was growing bored of his inactive life style; Kramer promised him a short working day, never filming after lunch, and Tracy agreed. The film also starred Sidney Poitier as the young black man with whom the daughter of a white liberal, Matt Drayton (Tracy), falls in love. Drayton's liberal principles are put to a test which, initially, they do not pass. He overcomes his objections to the marriage, however, and the scene in which he capitulates is particularly poignant for it turns into the final love scene he ever played with Katharine Hepburn. Drayton turns to his wife, played by Hepburn, and says, as his voice cracks, 'If what they feel for each other is even half what we felt, then that is everything.' After Tracy had spoken this line Hepburn burst into tears and many of the other people on the set also had tears in their eyes. Later critics commented on the scene's power. In *The New Yorker* Brendan Gill wrote:

When, at its climax, Mr Tracy turns to Miss Hepburn and tells her what an old man remembers, having loved, it is for us who are permitted to overhear him an experience that transcends the theatrical.

After completing the scene Tracy said to Kramer, 'You know, I read the script again last

Left: Tracy in *Guess Who's Coming to Dinner*. He died just ten days after filming was completed.

night, and if I were to die on the way home tonight, you can still release the picture with what you've got.' This remark shows that Tracy knew he did not have long to live. Indeed, this fact had probably already been brought home to him when insurance for him

Below: Spencer and Kate in *Guess Who's Coming to Dinner*. It was her decision, at the urging of Stanley Kramer, that the couple should make the film after Tracy had not worked for four years. She felt it would be good for him, and indeed it gave him a strong sense of purpose in his last days.

Above: In rehearsal for *Guess Who's Coming to Dinner.*

had been refused before production began. Both Kramer and Hepburn had to agree to forgo their salaries in the event of his being unable to finish the film and a replacement having to be found. As it was, Tracy was jubilant when he finished it, phoning several of his friends to share in his joy at having completed what he knew to be one of his finest films.

The critics agreed with him, praising the film as the best of the Kramer/Tracy collaborations, and the audiences concurred with the critics, as box office receipts testified. Both

Tracy and Hepburn were nominated for Academy Awards but Tracy was to be unaware of this, his ninth nomination, for 15 days after finishing production on the film he died. Early in the morning of June 10, 1967, Hepburn found him slumped on the kitchen table: he died before his doctor and his brother Carroll arrived on the scene. The official cause of death was pronounced by his doctor as being a massive heart attack. The funeral took place at the Immaculate Heart of Mary Catholic Church in Hollywood, the low requiem mass being said by Monsignor O'Donnell, Tracy's technical adviser on *Boys' Town*. Katharine Hepburn stayed away from the ceremony, probably in an attempt to persuade the press to stay away and therefore to afford Tracy a dignified burial. When she received the Oscar for best actress for her role in *Guess Who's Coming to Dinner*, she said that it was awarded to both her and Tracy as a team. In her autobiography she describes how on the morning of Tracy's funeral she drove to the funeral directors and helped lift his coffin on to the hearse. She said her final goodbye to him there, secretly and away from public glare, just as for so many years she and Tracy had conducted their love affair.

Spencer Tracy's death marked the closing stages of an era. Humphrey Bogart and Clark Gable, his contemporaries, had both died and Jimmy Cagney had retired. Tracy was the last of the great male movie stars of the 1930s and 1940s to give up making films. He had begun his film career in Hollywood's heyday when the studio system could make their stars small gods. Unlike the other male movie stars of the time, who maintained their popularity over a number of years, he did not always play himself. Bogart, Gable and Cagney were all effective actors if they played their own types of part. Tracy always insisted that he only ever played Spencer Tracy but his films prove testament against this. The Manuel of *Captains Courageous* is miles apart from Father Flanagan of *Boys' Town*. His later films show how, unlike his contemporaries, he was able to make the transition from romantic lead to a major character actor. It is impossible for mimics to imitate Tracy in the way they imitate Cagney and Bogart, and this is one reason why today Tracy is not so well known. His continuing reputation and popularity is due rather to his extraordinary acting ability and the lasting quality of the films in which he appeared. It is a reputation that he would be proud of.

Below: Stanley Kramer entertains Tracy, Hepburn and Oscar Werner on the set of *Guess Who's Coming to Dinner*. It was clear at the time that this would be Tracy's swansong, and Hepburn felt that she was awarded an Oscar on his account.

Filmography

Below: Publicity poster for *Libeled Lady*, one of the last of a series of lighweight comedies Spencer made in the 1930s.

1930
Up The River, DIR. John Ford, co-starring Humphrey Bogart, Claire Luce

1931
Quick Millions, DIR. Rowland Brown, co-starring Sally Eilers

Six-Cylinder Love, DIR. Thornton Freeland, co-starring Edward Everett Horton
Goldie, DIR. Benjamin Stoloff, co-starring Jean Harlow

1932
She Wanted A Millionaire, DIR. John Blystone, co-starring Joan Bennett
Sky Devils, DIR. Edward Sutherland, co-starring William Boyd, Ann Dvorak
Disorderly Conduct, DIR. John W Considine, co-starring Sally Eilers, Ralph Bellamy
Young America, DIR. Frank Borzage, co-starring Doris Kenyon, Ralph Bellamy
Society Girl, DIR. Sidney Lanfield, co-starring James Dunn, Peggy Shannon
Painted Woman, DIR. John Blystone, cc-starring William Boyd, Peggy Shannon
Me and My Girl, DIR. Raoul Walsh, co-starring Joan Bennett
Twenty Thousand Years in Sing Sing, DIR. Michael Curtiz, co-starring Bette Davis, Lyle Talbot

1933
Face in the Sky, DIR. Harry Lachman, co-starring Marian Nixon, Stuart Erwin
Shanghai Madness, DIR. John Blystone, co-starring Fay Wray, Ralph Morgan
The Power and the Glory, DIR. William K Howard, co-starring Colleen Moore, Ralph Morgan
The Mad Game, DIR. Irving Cummins, co-starring Claire Trevor, Ralph Morgan
A Man's Castle, DIR. Frank Borzage, co-starring Loretta Young

1934
Looking for Trouble, DIR. William Wellman, co-starring Jack Oakie
The Show-Off, DIR. Charles F Riesner, co-starring Madge Evans
Bottoms Up, DIR. David Butler, co-starring John Boles, Thelma Todd
Now I'll Tell, DIR. Edwin Burke, co-starring Helen Twelvetrees, Alice Faye

Marie Galante, DIR. Henry King, co-starring Ketti Gallian, Ned Sparks

1935

It's a Small World, DIR. Irving Cummins, co-starring Wendy Barrie

Murder Man, DIR. Tim Whelan, co-starring Virginia Bruce, Lionel Atwell

Dante's Inferno, DIR. Harry Lachman, co-starring Claire Trevor

Whipsaw, DIR. Sam Wood, co-starring Myrna Loy

1936

Riff Raff, DIR. J Walter Ruben, co-starring Jean Harlow

Fury, DIR. Fritz Lang, co-starring Sylvia Sidney, Walter Abel

San Francisco, DIR. W S Van Dyke, co-starring Clark Gable, Jeanette MacDonald

Libeled Lady, DIR. Jack Conway, co-starring Jean Harlow, William Powell, Myrna Loy

1937

They Gave Him A Gun, DIR. W S Van Dyke, co-starring Franchot Tone, Gladys George

Captains Courageous, DIR. Victor Fleming, co-starring Freddie Bartholomew, Lionel Barrymore

Big City, DIR. Frank Borzage, co-starring Luise Rainer

1938

Mannequin, DIR. Frank Borzage, co-starring Joan Crawford

Test Pilot, DIR. Victor Fleming, co-starring Clark Gable, Myrna Loy

Boys' Town, DIR. Norman Taurog, co-starring Mickey Rooney

1939

Stanley and Livingstone, DIR. Henry King, co-starring Sir Cedric Hardwicke

1940

I Take This Woman, DIR. W S Van Dyke, co-starring Hedy Lamarr

Northwest Passage, DIR. King Vidor, co-starring Robert Young

Edison the Man, DIR. Clarence Brown, co-starring Charles Coburn

Boom Town, DIR. Jack Conway, co-starring Clark Gable, Claudette Colbert, Hedy Lamarr

1941

Men of Boys' Town, DIR. Norman Taurog, co-starring Mickey Rooney

Dr Jekyll and Mr Hyde, DIR. Victor Fleming, co-starring Ingrid Bergman, Lana Turner

1942

Woman of the Year, DIR. George Stevens, co-starring Katharine Hepburn

Below: Publicity poster for *Thirty Seconds Over Tokyo*, a solid Second World War film about the planning of the first American attack on Japan.

Tortilla Flat, DIR. Victor Fleming, co-starring Hedy Lamarr, John Garfield

Keeper of the Flame, DIR. George Cukor, co-starring Katharine Hepburn

1943

A Guy Named Joe, DIR. Victor Fleming, co-starring Van Johnson, Irene Dunne

1944

The Seventh Cross, DIR. Fred Zinnemann, co-starring Signe Hasso, Hume Cronyn, Jessica Tandy

Thirty Seconds over Tokyo, DIR. Mervyn LeRoy, co-starring Van Johnson, Robert Walker

1945

Without Love, DIR. Harold S Bucquet, co-starring Katharine Hepburn

1947

The Sea of Grass, DIR. Elia Kazan, co-starring Katharine Hepburn, Melvyn Douglas

Cass Timberlane, DIR. George Sidney, co-starring Lana Turner

1948

State of the Union, DIR. Frank Capra, co-starring Katharine Hepburn, Angela Lansbury, Van Johnson

1949

Edward My Son, DIR. George Cukor, co-starring Deborah Kerr

Adam's Rib, DIR. George Cukor, co-starring Katharine Hepburn, Judy Holliday

1950

Malaya, DIR. Richard Thorp, co-starring James Stewart

Father of the Bride, DIR. Vincente Minnelli, co-starring Elizabeth Taylor, Joan Bennett, Don Taylor

Father's Little Dividend, DIR. Vincente Minnelli, co-starring Elizabeth Taylor, Joan Bennett, Don Taylor

1951

The People Against O'Hara, DIR. John Sturges, co-starring Pat O'Brien, Diana Lynn

Opposite: Tracy in 1939 with three of his favorite pets, Irish setters, on his ranch at Encino before leaving for Idaho to make *Northwest Passage*.

Below: With Hepburn, Van Johnson and Adolphe Menjou in a scene from *State of the Union*, in which he plays a presidential candidate.

1952
Pat and Mike, DIR. George Cukor, co-starring Katharine Hepburn

1953
Plymouth Adventure, DIR. Clarence Brown, co-starring Gene Tierney, Van Johnson
The Actress, DIR. George Cukor, co-starring Jean Simmons, Teresa Wright

1954
Broken Lance, DIR. Edward Dmytryk, co-starring Robert Wagner, Richard Widmark

1955
Bad Day at Black Rock, DIR. John Sturges, co-starring Robert Ryan, Anne Francis, Lee Marvin, Ernest Borgnine

1956
The Mountain, DIR. Edward Dmytryk, co-starring Robert Wagner

Below: Publicity poster for *Its a Mad Mad Mad Mad World*.

Above: Tracy with Katy Jurado in *Broken Lance*, in which he plays an autocratic cattle baron whose sons rebel against his overbearing ways.

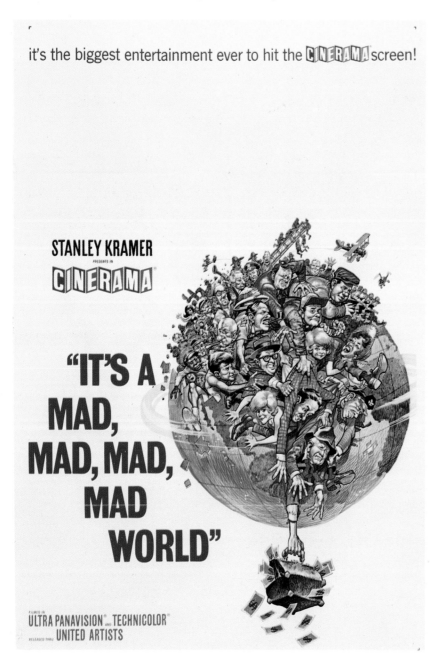

1957
Desk Set, DIR. Walter Lang, co-starring Katharine Hepburn, Joan Blondell, Dina Merrill

1958
The Old Man and the Sea, DIR. John Sturges, co-starring Felipe Pazes
The Last Hurrah, DIR. John Ford, co-starring Jeffrey Hunter, Pat O'Brien

1960
Inherit the Wind, DIR. Stanley Kramer, co-starring Fredric March, Gene Kelly

1961
The Devil at Four O'Clock, DIR. Mervyn LeRoy, co-starring Frank Sinatra
Judgment at Nuremberg, DIR. Stanley Kramer, co-starring Maximillian Schell, Richard Widmark, Burt Lancaster

1963
It's a Mad Mad Mad Mad World, DIR. Stanley Kramer, co-starring Milton Berle, Sid Caesar, Buddy Hackett, Ethel Merman, Mickey Rooney

1967
Guess Who's Coming to Dinner, DIR. Stanley Kramer, co-starring Katharine Hepburn, Sidney Poitier

Index

Figures in *italics* refer to illustrations

Academy awards *see* Oscars
Actress, The (1953) 58, 78
Adam, Mary *61*
Adam's Rib (1949) 6, 48, 50, *51*, *52*, *53*, *53*, 77
affair with Loretta Young 24
African Queen, The (1951) 55
Agee, James 47
alcoholism problems 6, 9-10, 13, 21, 23, 27, 30, 44, 62, 64
American Academy of Dramatic Art, New York 11
Anderson, Donna 65
Ashley, Elizabeth 69
awards *see* Oscars, Screen Writers' Guild

Baby Cyclone, The (play) 14, 15
Bad Day at Black Rock (1955) 58, 61, *61*, *62*, 78
Barnes, Howard 48
Barrymore, Lionel 33
Bartholomew, Freddie *14*, 33, *33*
Bellamy, Ralph 23
Bennett, Joan 21, *22*, 23, 54-55
Bergmann, Ingrid *34*
Big City (1937) 15, 34, 75
birth of Tracy 8
Blakiston, Jessie 44
Bogart, Humphrey 6, 17, *17*, *18*, 62, 73
Boom Town (1940) 37, 75
Borgnine, Ernest 58
Bottoms Up (1934) 74
Boyd, William 21
Boys' Club, The 23
Boys' Town (1938) 6, 35-36, *36*, *37*, 73, 75
Brennan, Walter 58, *61*
Broadway appearances 6, 11, 14, 15, 17, 19, 38, 44, 47
Broken Lance (1954) 58, 59, 62, 78, *78*
Brown, Johnny Mack *19*

Cagney, James 6, 21, 23, *23*, 61, 73
Cantwell, Archbishop J J *36*
Capra, Frank *34*
Captains Courageous (1937) 6, *14*, 30, 33-34, *33*, *34*, 36, 73, 75
Carrie B, ketch 33
Cass Timberlane (1947) 48, *48*
Catholicism 8, 24, 64
character roles, transition to 55, 73
character traits 6, 8
childhood of Tracy 8-9, *9*, *10*
Churchill, Marguerite *20*
Clift, Montgomery 68, 69
Cohan, George M 13, 14, *14*, 15
Colbert, Claudette 48
Conrad, William 59
Crawford, Joan 28, *32*, 33, 34
Cronyn, Hume *45*
Crowther, Bosley 53
Cukor, George 43, 55, 64
Curtis, Tony 65

Dante's Inferno (1935) 27, *27*, 75
Davis, Bette *37*
de Havilland, Olivia 36
deaf, Louise Tracy's work for 43-44, *44*
deafness of Tracy's son 13, 19, 43-44
death of Tracy 73
Demarest, William *61*

depression problems 13, 55
Desk Set (1957) 62, *63*, 78
Devil at Four O'Clock, The (1961) 67-68, 78
Disorderly Conduct (1932) 74
Dr Jekyll and Mr Hyde (1941) *34*, 37, 41, *50*, 75
drama training 11
Dunne, Irene 44, 47

Edgers, Kenneth 10
Edison the Man (1940) 36-37, 75
education of Tracy 8-10
Marquette Academy 10
Ripon College 10-11, debating team *10*, 11
Edward My Son (1949) 53, 77
Encino ranch *2*, 23, 44, *76*
Ericsson, John *62*
Evans, Madge *27*

Face in the Sky (1933) 74
family
brother, Carroll 8, 9, 10, 30, *33*, 73
daughter, Susie 15, 23, *23*
father, John 8, 9, 11, 15, 16
mother, Carrie 8, *11*
son, John 8, 13, 15, 19, 43-44, *44*, 47-48
wife, Louise Treadwell 8, 11-12, 13, *13*, 14-15, 16, 19, 23, 24, 26, 30, 34, *34*, 36, 43-44, *44*, 64, 69
Father of the Bride (1950) 54-55, *55*, 77
Father's Little Dividend (1950) 55, 56, 77
First World War 10
Flanagan, Father Edward J 35-36, *36*
Fleming, Victor 33
Ford, Henry *37*
Ford, John 6, 17
Fox Film Corporation 17, 19, 21, 24, 27
Fury (1936) 29-30, *30*, 75

Gable, Clark 6, 28, 29, *29*, 30, 34, 35, 37, 54, 55, 58, 62, 73
Garland, Judy 36, 68
Garrick, Richard *61*
Gill, Brendan 71
Goldie (1931) (original title *A Girl in Every Port*) 21, *21*, 74
Goodrich, Frances 54
Gordon, Ruth 53
Graham, Professor J Clark 11
Granger, Stewart 55
Grant, Cary 13, 38, *39*, 65
Great Depression (1929) 16, 19
Guess Who's Coming to Dinner (1967) 6, 69, 70, 71-73, *71*, *72*, *73*, 78
Guy Named Joe, A (1943) 44, *45*, 47, 54, 77

Hacker, Albert 54
Hardwicke, Sir Cedric *37*
Harlow, Jean 21, *21*, 28, *28*, 30, *32*
Hayward, Jim *61*
Hepburn, Katharine
background 38
early film career 38
films with Tracy *4-5*, 6, 38, *39*, 40, 41, *41*, 42, 43, 46, 47, *47*, 48, *49*, 50, *51*, *52*, 53, *53*, 55, 56, 58, 62, *63*, 70, 71, *71*, *72*, *73*, *73*, *77*
HUAC 48
Oscars 38, 73
relationship with Tracy 8, 27, 37, 41, 43, 44, 55, 62, 64, *64*, 65, 69, 73
stage appearances 38, 44, 47
Holliman, Earl 59

Hollywood 19, 21, 30, 36, 38, 44, 48, 54, 55, 64, 73
Houghton, Katharine 70
House Un-American Activities Committee (HUAC) 48, 55
Howard, Leslie 19
Hussey, Ruth 39
Hymer, Warren 16

I Take This Woman (1940) 15, 36, 75
Inherit the Wind (1960) 6, 65, *65*, 66, 67, 78
Irishmens' Club, The 23
It's a Mad Mad Mad Mad World (1963) 6, 68, 69, 78, *78*
It's a Small World (1935) 75

John Tracy Clinic for the Deaf 43-44, *44*
Johnson, Van 45, 47, *77*
Judgment at Nuremberg (1961) 6, 67, 68, 69, 78
Jurado, Katy 78

Kanin, Garson 53, 55-56, 65
Kanin, Michael 41
Kaufman, Millard 58
Kazan, Elia 48
Keeper of the Flame (1942) *42*, 43, *43*, 77
Kelly, Gene 54, 65, 67
Kelly, George 24
Kerr, Deborah 53
Kramer, Stanley 6, 65, 67, 68, 69, 71, 72, 73

Lamarr, Hedy 36
Lambs Club 14, 19
Lang, Fritz 29
Lardner Jr, Ring 41
Last Hurrah, The (1958) 62, 64, 78
Last Mile, The (play) 6, 16-17, 19
Leonard Wood stock company, White Plains, New York 11, 12, *12*
Libeled Lady (1936) 30, *32*, 74, 75
Lombard, Carole 19
Looking for Trouble (1934) 74
Loy, Myrna 28, 29, 30
Luce, Claire *17*, *18*

McCrystal, Margarite *27*
MacDonald, Jeanette 13, 28, *29*
McHugh, Frank 23
Mad Game, The (1933) 74
Malaya (1950) 77
Man Who Came Back, The (play) 11, *12*
Man's Castle, A (1933) 24, *24*, 74
Mankiewicz, Joe 41
Mannequin (1938) *32*, 34, 75
March, Fredric 66, 67
Marie Galante (1934) 75
Marquette Academy 10
marriage to Louise Treadwell 12
Marshall, E G *61*
Marty (1955) 58
Mayer, Louis B 28, 36, 41, 55
Me and My Girl (1932) 74
Men of Boys' Town (1941) 75
Menjou, Adolphe *77*
Merkel, Una 28
Metro Goldwyn Mayer (MGM) 24, 30, 36, 38, 44, 47, 53, 54, 55, 64, 65
signing up of Tracy 27, 28
partial contract with Tracy 56, 58
firing of Tracy 61, 62
Milwaukee (birthplace of Tracy) 8, 9
Moore, Colleen 24, *25*
Morgan, Frank 19, 23
Mountain, The (1956) 56, *61*, 62, 64, 78

Murder Man (1935) 28, 75

Never Let Me Go (1953) 55
New York 6, 11, 13, 14, 15, 19
Northwest Passage (1940) 36, 56, 75
Northwestern Military and Naval Academy, Lake Geneva, Wisconsin 10
Nothing But the Truth (play) 11
Now I'll Tell (1934) 74
Nugent, Frank S 30, 36

O'Brien, Pat 10, 11, 13, 14, 19, 23, 55, 62
O'Hara, John 58
Old Man and the Sea, The (1958) 60, 62, 78
Olivier, Laurence 6
Oscars
nominations for Tracy: 1936 (*San Francisco*) 30; 1950 (*Father of the Bride*) 55; 1955 (*Bad Day at Black Rock*) 58; 1958 (*The Old Man and the Sea*) 62; 1960 (*Inherit the Wind*) 67; 1967 (*Guess Who's Coming to Dinner*) 73
award won by Tracy: 1937 (*Captains Courageous*) 34, *34*; 1938 (*Boys' Town*) 36, *37*
special Oscar award to Tracy: Irving Thalberg award 1961 67
award won by Hepburn: 1933 (*Morning Glory*) 38; 1967 (*Guess Who's Coming to Dinner*) 73
Overman, Lynne 14, 23

Painted Woman (1932) 74
Pat and Mike (1952) 55-56, *56*, 58, 78
People Against O'Hara, The (1951) 55, 77
Philadelphia Story, The (play) 38
Philadelphia Story, The (film, 1940) 38, *39*
Pigeon, The (play) 11
Plymouth Adventure, The (1953) 56, 57, 78
Poitier, Sidney 65, *70*, 71
polo activities 8, 9, *18*, 19, *19*
Powell, William 28, 30
Power and the Glory, The (1933) 23-24, *25*, 74

Quick Millions (1931) *19*, *20*, 21, 74

Raft, George *19*
Rainer, Luise 15, *34*
Repertory Theater of Cincinnati 12
Riff Raff (1936) 28-29, *28*, 75
Ripon College 10-11, debating team *10*, 11
RKO 38
Robinson, Edward G 21
Rogers, Will *19*
romances 23, 24, 36
Rooney, Mickey 28, 36, 69
Royle, Selena 13, 14
R.U.R. (Rossum's Universal Robots) (play) 12
Rugged Path, The (play) 47

sailing activities 33
San Francisco (1936) 29-30, *29*, *31*, 75
Sargent, Franklin Havers 11
Schary, Dore 55
Screen Writers' Guild award 30
Sea of Grass, The (1947) *1*, 48, *49*, 77
Second World War 44, 47
Seventh Cross, The (1944) *45*, 47, 77
Shanghai Madness (1933) 74
She Wanted a Millionaire (1932) 21,

22, 74
Sheehan, Winfield 21, 24, 27
Sherwood, Robert Emmett 47
Ship of Fools (1965) 69
Show-Off, The (1934) 24, 27, 74
Simmons, Jean 58
Sinatra, Frank 54, 65, 68
Six-Cylinder Love (1931) 74
Sky Devils (1932) 74
Smith, Ludlow Ogden 38
Society Girl (1932) 74
Soldiers Three (1951) 55
Song and Dance Man, The (play) 13
stage appearances 6, 11, 12-14, 12, 14, 15, 16-17, 19, 47-48
Stanley and Livingstone (1939) 75
State of the Union, The (1948) 4-5, 38, 48, 77, 77
Sterling Motor Truck Company 8
Stewart, James 38, 39
stock companies 11, 12-14, 15

Strickling, Howard 61

Tandy, Jessica 45
Taylor, Elizabeth 55, 55
Test Pilot (1938) 34-35, 35, 75
Thalberg, Irving 28, 67
theatrical career 6, 11, 12-14, 12, 14, 15, 16-17, 19, 47-48
They Gave Him A Gun (1937) 75
Thirty Seconds over Tokyo (1944) 47, 75, 77
Tierney, Gene 57
Tortilla Flat (1942) 77
Treadwell, Louise, wife of Tracy 8, 11-12, 12, 13, 13, 14-15, 16, 19, 23, 24, 26, 30, 34, 34, 36, 43-44, 44, 64, 69
Trent Theater stock company, New Jersey 13-14
Trevor, Claire 61
Tribute to a Bad Man (1956) 61, 62

Troy, William 24
Troyat, Henri 56
Truth, The (play) 11
Tubelle, Larry 69
Turner, Lana 48, 48
Twentieth Century Fox 58
Twenty Thousand Years in Sing Sing (1932) 74
Two Girls and a Sailor (1944) 47

United States Navy, Tracy's World War I service in 10, 11
Up the River (1930) 6, 16, 17, 17, 18, 19, 74

Van Dyke II, W S 29

W H Wright's company, Grand Rapids, Michigan 13, 14, Lima, Ohio 15
Wagner, Robert 62

Warner Brothers 21
Watts Jr, Richard 19
Werner, Oscar 73
Whipsaw (1935) 29, 75
Whispering Friends (play) 15
Widmark, Richard 59
Wise, Robert 61
Without Love (play) 44, 47
Without Love (film, 1945) 46, 47, 47, 77
Woman of the Year (1942) 6, 39, 40, 41, 41, 42, 43, 50, 51, 75

Yearling, The (1946) 41
Yellow (play) 14, 15
York, Dick 65
Young, Loretta 24, 24
Young America (1932) 74

Zimbalist, Sam 61
Zinnemann, Fred 60, 62

ACKNOWLEDGMENTS

The publisher would like to thank Martin Bristow, who designed this book; Sara Dunphy for picture research; and Jessica Orebi Gann, the editor. We are also grateful to the following institutions and agencies for permission to reproduce illustrative material.

Bettmann Archive: 1, 9 (bottom), 12 (top), 13, 18 (top), 22, 23 (top), 24, 25, 26, 27 (both), 32 (top), 33 (both), 34 (bottom), 36 (bottom), 41, 42 (bottom), 44 (bottom), 45 (top), 48, 49, 53 (bottom), 61 (both), 69, 73, 76
Brompton Picture Library: 7, 8, 14 (bottom), 15 (top), 28, 31, 39 (both), 40 (both), 42 (top), 43, 45 (bottom), 50 (both), 51, 53 (top), 54, 55, 56 (bottom), 57, 58, 59 (both), 62, 63 (both), 67 (bottom), 68, 70 (top), 71 (both), 78 (both).
Photofest: 2, 9 (top), 11, 16 (bottom), 21, 70 (bottom), 74, 75
Ripon College Archives: 10 (bottom)
Springer-Bettmann Film Archive: 16, 17 (top), 18 (bottom), 19 (top), 20, 29, 30, 32 (bottom), 35, 36 (top), 46, 47, 52, 56 (top), 60, 64, 65, 77
University of Texas: 12 (bottom), 14 (top)
UPI/Bettmann: 4-5, 6, 10 (top), 19 (bottom), 23 (bottom), 34 (top), 37 (both), 38, 44 (top), 66, 67 (top), 72